The One in the Many

Also by David Ignatow

Poems

The Gentle Weight Lifter

Say Pardon

Figures of the Human

Earth Hard: Selected Poems (1968)

Rescue the Dead

Poems 1934–1969

The Notebooks of David Ignatow

Selected Poems (1975)

Open Between Us (prose)

New and Collected Poems 1970–1985

David Ignatow

The One in the Many

A Poet's Memoirs

Wesleyan University Press
Middletown, Connecticut

© 1988 by David Ignatow

Acknowledgments are made to New Directions Publishing Corp. for permission to reprint "Patterson" and "Convivio" by William Carlos Williams (*The Collected Later Poems of William Carlos Williams*, New Directions, 1963) and "The Trees," also by William Carlos Williams (*The Collected Earlier Poems of William Carlos Williams*, New Directions, 1986); to Carcanet Press for permission to reprint "The Trees" by William Carlos Williams (*The Collected Poems 1909–1939*, A Walton Litz and Christopher MacGowan, eds., Carcanet Press Limited, 1987); and to Alfred A. Knopf, Inc. for permission to reprint "The Emperor of Ice Cream," "United Dames of America," and "Notes Toward a Supreme Fiction," by Wallace Stevens (*The Collected Poems of Wallace Stevens*, Alfred A. Knopf, 1969).

See page 195 for further acknowledgments.

All inquiries and permissions requests should be addressed to the Publisher, Wesleyan University Press, 110 Mt. Vernon Street, Middletown, Connecticut 06457

Library of Congress Cataloging-in-Publication Data
Ignatow, David, 1914–
    The one in the many: a poet's memoirs/David Ignatow.—1st ed.
        p.   cm.
    Includes index.
    ISBN 0–8195–5211–9
    1. Ignatow, David, 1914–   —Biography.   2. Poets, American—20th
century—Biography.   I. Title.
PS3517.G53Z473   1988
811'.54—dc 19
[B]   88–19804
                                                                       CIP

Manufactured in the United States of America

FIRST EDITION

Contents

vi   Contents

Foreword

What the reader will come upon is writing conceived and written over a period spanning four decades, beginning with the fifties and continuing through the present. Yet the writing in all four decades holds to a common theme. I was surprised, reading through the manuscript to prepare for its publication in book form. But I was wrong to be surprised. As I looked back across the decades, I sensed, even if vaguely, an underlying need directing my writing. For example, if I were commissioned today to write an article or give a talk—both served as stimulants for these writings over the years—I would concentrate on the theme that has preoccupied my literary life and thought through four decades, that is, the need to reveal to myself the substructure of aesthetic theory and its practice—in other words, its human dimension.

I have been, of course, motivated by my own circumstances— that much I know—of doubts, questions, assertions, affirmations, and at times rejection and anger. For in none of these reactions could I find satisfaction is discussing theory as theory alone. I had to present each reaction in its time, place, and case in relation to the practice of the poetics of the decade. Each developed its unique theoretical debate, to which I gave voice in an essay or lecture or poem, but my awareness of the human factor that lay beneath the surface of an aesthetic practice dominated everything I wrote.

As I saw this body of writing suggest itself as a whole, it led me to attempt to fulfill that intent. I have strengthened and underlined my theme by certain editorial changes. For example, I have eliminated unrelated introductory remarks, dated references, repetitions, and overlapping materials, but more urgently, I have also revised and/or enlarged upon a subject where I saw it needed further clarification and information to round out the sense of the whole. I have included several unpublished essays, as well as sections from my *Notebooks,* to further emphasize the book's overarching theme.

In my efforts through the decades to seek for the substructure of aesthetic decisions and practices, I know I have voyaged in dark waters of motivation in the author under discussion, motivation obscure to him or that he is unaware of or unwilling on the face of it to acknowledge, but that is where I found my interest and stimulation. Perhaps at the same time it revealed me to others in the process. Well, so be it, since, for me, that is an incentive to write truthfully and well, at least to try to, for my own satisfaction and pride.

I conclude on a metaphorical note. Many visiting the countryside or living in it, as I do, have observed the fragile marshes and been struck by the many lush stretches where fish and birds thrive in what we often consider slimy waste places. Yet from these so-called waste places emerge well-nourished birds and fish to make their way among their own kind to fulfill their life's being. The cycle repeats itself over and over again, and we come to admire, respect and even revere the process of decay and regeneration in the chemistry of the marshes for what it says to us about our own fragile beginnings. May the reader think of these marshes as the image of what he or she will find in these hard-written pages.

Here I may be permitted to name the distinguished friends and colleagues to whom I owe a debt of gratitude for their advice, suggestions, criticisms, and editorial acumen with which these essays and memoirs were able to take their final form. I name them in alphabetical order, for there is no standard by which each can be measured for his or her unique contribution: Robert Bly, Rose Graubart, Milton Hindus, Hank Lazer, Jerome Mazzaro, Ralph J. Mills, Jr., Stanley Moss, Roy Harvey Pearce, Harvey Shapiro, and Virginia R. Terris. But especially do I thank Jeannette Hopkins, without whose care and help this book would not have come to be.

The first part of Chapter 5 was written in 1962 in response to a request from the Department of English at Vassar College for a statement; the latter part was written for high school and elementary school classes at the request of the Academy of American Poets. Chapter 6 was read in 1981 as an address to the Department of English at York College, CUNY. Chapter 7 was read at the Walt Whitman Birthplace Association, at Barnard College, and at the Poet's House in New York. Chapter 12 was read in 1986 at the memorial meeting for Paul Blackburn at New York University. Chapter 13 was read at the Donnell Library as an introduction for the Academy of American Poets. The latter part of Chapter 18 was read at the Guggenheim Museum as an introduction to a reading sponsored by the Academy of American Poets. Chapter 19, originally titled "In Memoriam: Paul Zweig, 1935–1984," first appeared in the Fall 1984 *Newsletter* of the Poetry Society of America.

D. I.
East Hampton, N.Y.
March 3, 1988

I. The One in the Many

1. The Formative Years

My first memory at about age four was of standing in a dark vestibule during the day and being admonished by my mother for wanting to leave the house to play in the street with my friends. I had lived through a scarlet fever crisis not long before and was still recovering. It was 1918, and scarlet fever was raging through the country. I had come through safely one night when no one was certain that I would survive until the next morning. Now I was restless with nothing to divert my mind from my illness, but my mother had to threaten that the "ambulance" would come to take me away if I insisted on leaving the house. The idea of an "ambulance," something so intimidating and mysterious, was enough to quiet me, and I resigned myself to waiting.

My next memory is of descending the stairs a bit shakily, feeling the carpet beneath my feet as if I were walking on air. In the street, to my delight, there was a tall boy who I felt I knew from the past waiting to give me a tricycle as a gift. It was a used one, its paint scratched or missing in places, but he was smiling down on me with such a kindly look that I knew, even before he handed me the bike, that he meant something good, and the bike made it fact, an overwhelming fact by which I felt loved as I could not remember ever before having experienced. I climbed on to the seat of the bike and began to peddle back and forth up and down the block, left alone to enjoy myself. Not much later I became bored with the bike. It could only do one thing over and over, and that did not seem enough for me. I had explored all the possibilities, first sitting behind the wheel for several rides back and forth, then climbing down and mounting up on the lower rear axle and pushing forward while holding on to the handlebars. That was all that was possible to keep my interest, and it was not enough.

Bored, I looked around and noticed that the same friend who had given me the bike was standing with a group of other boys around a small fire up against the curb across the street. I ventured over to join him, although feeling shy about joining boys so much older than I. They treated me kindly, as my tall friend smiled down at me. At first the others seemed a bit put out at my presumption at wanting to join as an equal. It might have made them feel as though they were being brought back to my age and size, but my friend, by welcoming me, made them feel they could treat me as a guest without harm to their own status, and so I was privileged to listen in on a discussion about ladybugs that lit on one's hand, blown there by a breeze. They were proclaiming that a ladybug was a harbinger of rain. Later I looked for ladybugs, and when one did alight on me or nearby I would chant what I had learned from the boys around the fire: "Ladybug, ladybug, fly away, please come back another day."

My family was then living in Brooklyn in an apartment on the first floor of a house occupied also by my father's older brother, Israel, who lived on the ground floor next door to his hardware store. He owned the house. He also owned mortgages of many houses similar to this one in the neighborhood. He was a wealthy man by our standards. One day, coming home from kindergarten I think, I climbed the one flight to our apartment and found the door locked. I climbed down and waited for my mother's return. She was shopping, I believed. About an hour went by, and I began to cry. When she finally arrived, my face was completely bathed in tears, and my mother was alarmed. She gave me a package of fresh herring wrapped in old newspaper to take up to the apartment. It was a gesture to soothe my feelings and to show me that I was still part of her concerns, if not the most important part, and that I was still with her in her thoughts, even if she could not be with me at all times. As I reached the top of the stairs, my mother already at the door to the apartment, my foot slipped. I lost my balance and came tumbling down the flight of stairs, head over heels, but still holding on to the herring. I received a cut between my eyebrows that to this day is visible. I remember the fall in connection with my mother's absence; it tells me something about the sense of loss and unhappiness I learned then and there.

We moved from that apartment, I believe, soon after the First World War. I had liked that apartment and remember it as airy and sunny but with a vestibule without a window, where I stood to be admonished by my mother. We moved to 44th Street in the immediate neighborhood, one short block away. We were moving into a house my father had bought with a loan from his brother Israel. It had been bought on speculation. Besides our apartment, there were five others occupied by strangers who paid rent to my father. My uncle wanted to see my father prosper in the bindery business as he did himself in hardware. My father was his favorite brother. There were four brothers, including Israel. Each had come over from Kiev on a separate trip. They had managed to bring over their mother, who alternated living with each of the four in turn. There was also a sister, married to a butcher and living in the Bronx. The house my father bought was on a Boro Park street dominated by Italian families of low middle- and working-class income.

We moved into our new home, and my troubles with the Italian boys my age began. They played a rough game of Throwing Association, in which the football was thrown between two sides of supposedly equal numbers of players, with the side that received the ball attempting to run past the opposite team to reach a certain point on the street marked as the goal. The game resembled football except that there was no kicking of the ball, no tackling, and no body blocking. The Italian boys ignored the rules, especially when playing with us, a team made up of the few Jews that had come to live on this street. Sometimes during the game, when I, as the fastest runner on my team, had the ball in my hands, the Italian boys tried desperately to block me. I would manage to avoid them at top speed. But one day, after they had apparently

talked it over among themselves, one who thought himself fast too
did manage to run alongside me as I was carrying the ball, and he
threw himself at my shoulder, forcing me up on the sidewalk and
nearly causing me to fall. I righted myself in time. That told me
that things would be getting worse very soon. It was to be my last
game of Throwing Association in competition with these boys.

To occupy myself after school, following homework, rather
than venture into the street to risk another and perhaps even worse
assault, I took to reading. It soon possessed me, especially books
of adventure: the Tom Swifts, the Frank and Dick Merriwells, the
Nick Carters, any books about travel by air, by train, by ship to
dangerous lands amidst plots and intrigues of bad men against
good men—morality versus immorality, that is, lying as against
telling the truth, and especially about living up to one's code of
honorable conduct toward one's equals and toward those in partic-
ular who needed help. I was learning ethics in a most exciting way.

Several years went by in this pleasant, nearly paradisal way—all
in my head. I had begun to put on weight through my sedentary
habit of reading at the window, where from time to time I looked
out upon the street to see the Italian boys playing among them-
selves as violently as ever and sometimes quarreling and swinging
fists. It was not my style. It was not how I had been raised and,
anyway, I had begun to love school. It gave me a sense of the im-
portance of being a child, one on whom money and care were
being spent to teach me how to become an adult. I wanted to be-
come an adult quickly, the thought of the books I was reading at
home spurring me on. I was to become indifferent to the Italian
boys, though guarded on passing them on my way to the library
as they played their games. I was alert to any chance that perhaps
one or two might turn to me and make a dash at me. To make
myself inconspicuous, I would walk with my eyes facing ahead,
the books tucked under my arm, which then gave the appearance
of a crippled arm, so that I would be thought of as too helpless to
be a threat. I walked without once glancing in their direction. I

think it was their will to have it so too. Since they had decided among themselves that they did not want to play with Jewish boys, they would ignore us. In that way, should we try to join them again, they could feign ignorance of us and reject us, as if we did not exist. It suited me too, now that I had found so much pleasure and excitement in books and in school lessons.

The new house we lived in had no central heating, except for a large coal-burning stove in the kitchen on which my mother cooked. In winter, when time came for bed, we took with us heated flatirons wrapped in towels to place at our feet under the cold sheets in the cold room. We'd fall asleep silently, to awaken to rooms turned icy overnight and run swiftly in our nightshirts into the kitchen where my mother would have the stove burning brightly. I remember her as stoical and active in her silence.

Several years passed and my father sold the house for a profit. It may have been the year 1921, possibly 1922, as the stock market began to pick up speed. We moved to a newly built neighborhood that had taken over farmland that was still there in the Maplewood section of Brooklyn. A pumpkin farm stood right across the street. There were no worn brick-faced buildings anywhere in sight like those that lined 44th Street between 13th and 14th Avenues, where we had been living.

Thirteenth Avenue, whenever I found myself on it on an errand for my mother, recalled earlier days when my father owned and operated a butcher shop, a block away from one owned by his next oldest brother, Philip. Philip had urged my father to open this butcher shop, after my father had been blackballed from the bookbinding industry for leading a strike against the owner of the shop. My father had been in a secure position that paid a good salary; he was the foreman, the extended arm and authority of the boss. He was not supposed to side with the workers, but my father, a Social Democrat from the old days in Kiev, had his principles. The workers knew of his association with the Social Democrats in Kiev and of his narrow escape from Russia during the counter-revolution of 1905, and so they secretly appealed to him, complaining of their long hours of work without decent wages. The bindery workers' union was in its infancy. My father, finding himself in sympathy with the pains and tribulations of the workers, led the strike to force a union on the boss. The strike apparently was becoming effective when the boss and the strikers met secretly behind my father's back, so to speak, and agreed upon a settlement, which gave the strikers their union scale and working hours but on the condition that my father be fired from his job as foreman for having violated his relationship to his boss. He was also barred from returning as an ordinary worker. This plan was agreed upon by the workers, who knew little or nothing at that time of union solidarity, and my father found himself unable to find another job in the industry. Desperate for work, he took the advice to open a butcher shop virtually next door to Philip's. My uncle would be in a position to guide my father in a business unfamiliar to him in many ways.

I went on errands for my father in the morning before attending school and in the evening after having done my homework hastily, under pressure to take orders from customers at their homes. In the morning I would deliver packages of meat and/or chickens to customers who had ordered them the night before. In the evening I would make the rounds of these same customers to take their orders for the next day. I couldn't have been more than seven years old. My school studies suffered, especially after my mother had to leave for a gallstone operation. It kept her in the hospital for about a month at least, I think. Her long, long absence seemed interminable. My sister had to be housed with a relative in the Bronx, while I stayed with my father.

When my mother finally returned home, the school term had already ended. I was "put back," having failed in all subjects and with a notice that I had lice in my hair. Lice were the plague of all butcher shops, especially those that dealt in chickens, and I delivered chickens to customers or collected them freshly slaughtered in a paper bag from the market. My father was terribly angry at my failing report card and, in my mother's presence, that very evening she returned from the hospital, raised his hand to strike me. I was sure that my father, if he had not been so exhausted, the chicken feathers still clinging to his wrists and his hands smeared with blood, would have understood the cause of my failure. I loved him and felt I understood him, but I was frightened of his trigger temper. My mother stepped between us and in a gentle voice admonished my father, making him understand that the failure could only have been caused by her absence and his consequent neglect of me. He lowered his hand. I certainly was relieved to see my mother back at last. That evening I got my first thorough bath and hair wash in a long while, and it was, for once, a deep pleasure.

I continued to be sent by my father on regular missions to the chicken market. I would stand by the barrel into which the slaughtered chickens would be dropped and watch the rabbi, with one hand, grab a live one by the throat from out of the crate in which many more were squawking and treading restlessly, as if sensing something ominous about to happen. In the other hand he held a knife, which he drew swiftly across the chicken's throat. The chicken gasped for air. The rabbi with his finger flipped out one end of the windpipe so that the blood could flow freely, then tossed the chicken into the barrel to bleed out its life. When the number of chickens ordered by my father had been slaughtered and drained of their blood at the bottom of the barrel, the rabbi placed them in a huge brown paper bag. It was a weekly ritual, which I had begun to look forward to with a kind of fascination touched with horror. Besides, it got me away from the shop to see new sights and streets. It was worth the trip to the market to witness the busy coming and going of people, trucks, cars, with speech loud or private among people on busy 13th Avenue. I was learning something of how life was being lived by others. One of my best poems written in later years, "Ritual One," published in *Rescue the Dead,* is filled with that atmosphere.

And so, I already felt as a child that I had a sad life ahead of me. One winter day, as I was about to deliver an order, I found a sparrow lying still on the ground across the street from my father's shop. I tucked the bird into one of the side pockets of my coat, hoping, perhaps really wanting to expect, that the warmth of my pocket would revive the bird. I thought about it as I went about my errand, not daring to look into my pocket for fear of being disappointed, and when I returned to the spot where I had found the bird, I removed it from my pocket, fearful though still wanting to hope, for even then I sensed, having watched the chickens die, that death was final and absolute. The bird in my hand lay still, and for some reason I felt it was something for me to always remember, and so I determined to give it a fitting burial. I dug a hole beside the concrete sidewalk in the dirt section meant for trees or bushes. I dug deep so that the bird, I felt, would have the dignity of its rest undisturbed by a dog or cat, as it deserved for having tried to live through the winter.

At last—after a long agonizing period for him, my mother, and me—my father returned to the bindery business, the blackballing having been lifted or forgotten. He was, after all, a highly skilled worker, and there was now a great demand for workers of his ability in the growing bindery business. He had given up the butcher shop as a failure. A rivalry had grown up between the two brothers over customers each was drawing from the other. Even I as a child could sense that the good will of my father's brother could not last long when it came to a question of losing business that was originally his. My mother, who worked behind the counter, one day strode out of the butcher shop, with a meat cleaver in her hand, and headed toward my uncle's shop where his wife also was employed. She was going to use the cleaver on her sister-in-law after having heard from one of the customers an insulting remark about her that her sister-in-law had made in front of customers. It had been quickly related to my mother by eager but shocked hearers. My father dashed out of the shop to turn my mother back in the presence of horrified onlookers. Working in the store, my mother would become exhausted, suffering from aching and cold legs and toes during winter. For a woman of her gentle, mild temperament to reach for a meat cleaver to use on her sister-in-law came as a shock to me, and I sensed in my childish way something vaguely terrifying beneath the surface of people's lives.

I believe it was after that incident that my father determined to sell the business and find his way back to bindery work, his life's training, an art he had learned as a child apprentice to a gentile binder of fine books with fine bindings. After his apprenticeship, he had been hired out to the Kiev monastery where, ironically, he read the forbidden, censored books, such as those of Marx, Lenin, Bukharin, and Plekhanov, and those that were barely tolerated, such as Gorky, Tolstoy, and Chekhov. It was his one and only time for education, and it was the education of a radical in the refuge of a monastery.

Back in the bindery business, and having sold the cold-water six-apartment tenement building in its working-class neighborhood, he was upward bound at last, about to move into a new two-family brick house with all modern improvements: steam heat, hot running water, electricity, and a garage for a possible car one day—all of the amenities promised by American standards. His wealthy older brother Israel was behind this move too, having promised to help my father with money if he were to run short after investing in this new house the profit he had made from selling the old one. Israel had already moved his family into this same new neighborhood, into a similar kind of house around the corner. He was intent on having his younger brother near him and in an equally prosperous condition.

This new, red-brick house was a disappointment to me. It did not have the gable roof I had read about in so many books about the two Merriwell heroes, who lived in large frame houses with gable roofs, large attics, and front porches surrounded by wide lawns of grass and trees. This red-brick house was absolutely identical to all the others on its street. I realized that to find my way back to my house when returning from school or from an errand for my mother I would have to count the houses to be sure which was my own. I was very disappointed, and I believe I said so under my breath to my younger sister, who was seated beside me in the moving van as we arrived at the house. It was my first disillusionment after having been raised to believe in and look forward to the ideal American life, as lived by Frank and Dick Merriwell, my ideal heroes at age eleven.

There's much I could tell about what I learned and lived through in this house, but nothing else compares to the climactic episodes between my father and me that followed my graduation from high school. I was determined to become a writer. Several of my English teachers had been quite flattering about my ability to write. It all really began in junior high school, where we were asked to write an imaginative composition about anything we wished. I wrote of a civil war scene at night, of camp fires on both sides of the battleground that resembled stars. The description went on for a full page. The teacher wrote on it "very vivid," and other complimentary phrases. She read the paper aloud in class. To this day, I cannot recall how and where I conceived of such a description. Had I read something like it in a book? The scene was not one I had copied. It had been written by a student reaching for effects. My pride in my accomplishment began after reading her remarks and hearing her read from my paper. My spirit soared. It was as if already I was launched on my career as a writer.

In high school, two English teachers also took notice of me, one openly in front of the class, inviting me to go with her to hear Robert Frost read from his poems at the New School for Social Research in Manhattan. It was a challenge to me to declare myself in front of class, an embarrassing thing when one wanted to fit in with the others, to make friends and keep them. At first I demurred, but when she retorted, "Are you hiding your light under a bushel?" I immediately gave in. At the reading, I found myself unable to understand the poems Frost was reading. They were beyond me, much as I was drawn to the voice in which they were read. It was the voice of another kind of world. It was a settled, gravelly kind of voice that seemed to have grown up out of soil, unlike the voice I was used to hearing at home—high-pitched and filled with anxiety, especially the voice of my father. My mother, on the other hand, who at times would be aggrieved by the actions of her two daughters or by me, spoke only with firmness. Yet another teacher often smiled at me in class in my next term, apparently having heard of my trip to hear Frost, the only student to do so in the entire school.

I gathered from all these attentions that I was cut out for a special life, that of writer, different from everyone else among my friends in school and at play in the neighborhood. My sense of it was capped by Maurice Zolotow, a senior at the school and then editor of the school magazine. He came to class one day to solicit work for the magazine, and I set about writing a piece. Zolotow took it, but I did not know about it until weeks later when I found it, to my surprise, printed in the pages of the magazine, then being distributed in class. It was, coincidentally, the first semester of my senior year and but four months to graduation. If I had been fearful of becoming a writer because of the hardships I already sensed in the real world and in my family life, seeing my first publication in an actual magazine resolved the issue for me: I would become a writer against any odds.

Before long, however, a conflict arose between my father and me as a result of the advent of the Great Depression of 1929. I was still attending high school. My father had invested virtually all his profit from the sale of the tenement building in the purchase of this new house; and, with what was left, he invested in opening a bindery business of his own in partnership with a fellow binder. In 1928, everything looked good. A year earlier I had been confirmed as an adult on my thirteenth birthday, as is the ritual in the Jewish religion. It gave much pleasure and satisfaction to my parents, but the ritual itself took place in a shabby store at 6 A.M. and was hurried through to get my father to his job on time. My father then was still an employee of a bindery but earned a fine salary from which he managed to put aside a bit for savings. In 1928, he joined with his binder friend in their new venture, and all was going well; but 1929 was the year of the American economy's total collapse, and his business began to sink. There was no money in reserve. He had to borrow further from his brother to stay afloat. Things became even more desperate. I was old enough to work as a messenger or handy person for one of the large stores. I went reluctantly to Wanamaker's in Manhattan, remembering my past failures at school, but I was under pressure from my father and from my mother's revelation to me, privately, that the money I would earn would help tide her over with the expenses of the house. I worked weekends, missing out on the fun many of my friends in the neighborhood were having among themselves on Saturdays and Sundays—playing ball, going to the movies, joining in small parties at home. My sadness told on my face, and my mother tried to comfort me.

The money I earned also helped pay my carfare and lunches at school; and so I felt a certain satisfaction when I boarded a bus for school and when I put down money for a sandwich and milk there. My father's business grew less and less stable, however. Through my mother he began to press me to leave school and take the place of a worker in his shop so that my salary could help pay the expenses of the house—the mortgage, for one thing, and the loan from his brother. Israel had begun to insist on payment, himself strapped in the Depression. I could feel the tension in the air between my parents and in my father's conduct toward me— nothing openly; he was yet too self-conscious of this contradiction with his conduct toward me in the past. Finally, my mother put her foot down—she would do what was necessary in the house to cut expenses, such as giving up the apartment janitor. She would take over the job of shoveling coal into the furnace and of removing the barrels of ashes. She would do the laundry herself instead of sending it out. My father backed off, appalled by her offer but unable to refuse; he himself took on the job of the worker he had wanted me to replace, and so added to his own work. In other words, he would take my place in the shop until I was ready to step in after graduating from high school. Some of my poems, published and unpublished, deal with these episodes, many written at the time, others in retrospect but in a tone mainly of sorrow and contemplation, a far change from the Shelleyian exaltations of my earlier poems.

At my graduation from high school, my view of myself as a writer was already formed. It was, ironically, my father's own interest in literature that had originally encouraged me to become a writer. When I was quite small, perhaps ten, I would stand at his knee and listen to him recite the stories by Russian authors he had read in the Kiev monastery. He would never tire of praising them to me and of speaking of them with a rapture that I equated with love. I began to believe that to win my father's love I too would have to become a writer whom he could praise. My speech at my bar mitzvah ceremony, written by me with his smiling permission, gave him quiet pleasure and pride in me in front of his relatives seated around the table and listening. Yet here now, some years later, he was demanding that I give up all he had inspired in me to enter his bindery to work long hours that he knew would exhaust me and give me no chance to write.

One incident may illuminate the struggle that arose between us, a story I have not yet told elsewhere. I was already at work in his shop, having had to bow to circumstance. One day I left earlier than usual, rebellious in my frustration. I came home, had my dinner, and went to my room to write, with the door locked. My father arrived several hours later in a rage, shouting that he was going to throw me out of the house that night. I came from my room grimly to face him and have it out once and for all, come what may. I had been tortured to the breaking point by the heavy, endless, repetitive work at his bindery, without a word of sympathy from him, he who knew what I had been planning for myself once out of high school and who at one time had taken pride and pleasure in my writing. We stood face to face in the kitchen, exchanging words and about to come to blows. I watched my father's face contort and his body tense as he began to raise his arm to strike me. My mother, horrified, stepped in between us, as she had when I failed at school as a boy of seven.

Yet there was another incident, in a way amusing and perhaps ironic too. Working at one of the folding machines, I had become friendly with the young chief mechanic, Henry, somewhat older than I, who complained to me privately that he was not earning enough. Elsewhere there were union shops in which workers of his status received a much higher wage than his. My father now hated unions, especially the Binders' Union, the one he associated with the workers who had betrayed him years ago. I was sympathetic to Henry and, like my father in his time, counseled my friend to bring the union into the shop to force my father to make a contract with it. One day my father fired me and ordered me home where he would "have a talk with me." I instantly knew what he meant by the look on my friend's face as he heard me being fired. Henry, for some reason known only to himself, had told my father of my counsel, and I was out of a job, in fact a scoundrel and a potential patricide. I enjoyed the idea of being thrown out of the shop, but I had only done what my father himself had done years ago. I had modeled myself on him, and with the same result, strangely enough. I was ordered back a week later. Henry had received a raise, but was a very subdued young man in his relations with me.

My mother grew up illiterate, even in her own languages, Yiddish and Ukrainian. Her father, a woodsman for the Austro-Hungarian government, did not believe in educating his two daughters. It was the rule in those days, and so my mother spent her youth in the country, ignorant but content with the beauty of the forest and its peacefulness. My father taught her to read Yiddish from the *Jewish Forward*, his favorite newspaper, a Socialist organ of the party to which he had belonged in Russia. It was his favorite paper for reasons other than its principles; he was interested in the writers who contributed to it, though he ignored the paper's editorials and slanted news. I can still see my mother kneeling upon a chair and leaning over the newspaper spread out upon the kitchen table, laboriously making out the words on the page. I took her as a model of calm and perseverance.

During the Depression, my father tried to live on fifty cents a day. That was actually all he could allow himself. With that fifty cents he paid his carfare, bought his lunch of soup and bread, and purchased a newspaper. For twelve hours a day until he could come home he would have to survive on that one meal. He'd be starved, strained, and near hysteria from exhaustion. One day, as I was seated in the living room from which I could look into the kitchen, I saw my father suddenly lift his hand and strike my mother on the face. There had been words between them, my mother speaking forthrightly, without raising her voice. I couldn't believe my eyes. He had never before attempted nor probably ever thought himself capable of such a thing. I was deeply angry and distressed. I knew of the high bills my mother owed to the grocer and to the butcher. Several times she had been refused further food unless she came forth with some payment on the debt. I could overhear the conversation between them at other times. Matters at the stores may have become worse, and she may have been threatened with a complete cutoff. My parents may have been talking about money, and she may have insisted upon getting more from him, little that he had to spare from wages to his workers and for supplies in the shop. Exhausted as he was from overwork and from lack of a good diet, he had let his temper get the best of him. I saw my mother hold her cheek and look at him. Nothing further was said between them. They parted, and I remained seated, unable to move, unable to think of what to do, if anything. The image of my father, as I remembered him from my childhood, one to laugh and invite me on walks with him of a Sunday—all that vanished. Here was a man to be wary of, to guard against, to get away from as soon as possible. For my mother I felt grief. She was in a hopeless position.

One afternoon after arriving from school, I came upon her washing clothes in a kitchen tub. A scrubbing board had been stuck into the suds over which she was leaning and scrubbing away at the clothes against the board, a strained, energetic expression on her face. She looked up at me with an expression that was sad but contained.

In 1934, when I was twenty, I received an invitation to join the Writers Project of the WPA organized under the Roosevelt administration for writers in need. The invitation came as a result of my first story in a small literary magazine called *New Talent*. The story had been listed among the Honorable Mentions of the 1933 O. Henry Collection of Best Short Stories of that year. I had managed to write it in the time between late dinner and sleep after my work at the bindery. The story was about an aging mother being watched by her young son as she rocked herself back and forth in silence at a window. One weekend afternoon sometime before the story's publication, as we two sat in the sun parlor, I let my mother know how I felt about working in my father's shop. It was spoken in a tone of voice that deeply distressed her. I was feeling that my life had become hopeless, much like hers. She quickly promised to speak to my father to see whether he could ease the number of working hours for me. I had no hope that it could be done, knowing of the desperate fight he was waging against going broke.

The arrival of the letter of invitation suddenly put new light on the whole situation. We, my mother and I, put our heads together and, with some quick thinking on her part, arrived at a plan that would qualify me for the WPA job, since the bureaucracy required evidence above and beyond qualification as a writer. To be hired, a writer had to be in proven need according to WPA regulations. I had first to qualify for Home Relief as an indigent person. At my mother's suggestion, I was "boarding" at my aunt's apartment as a complete stranger to her and about to be evicted for lack of rent. The plan worked smoothly, and within a week I was qualified to accept the offer on the Writers Project. No one was more relieved than my mother. To me, the success of the outcome simply had been long overdue. I was excited, of course, but I could also feel my life coming together at last. My father, of necessity, had been apprised of the plan, and when it came through successfully he was silent, as though he now could breathe freely himself, rid of his guilt toward me. At any rate, I was to give a part of my salary to help pay the expenses of the house, though I already had plans to live elsewhere, in Greenwich Village. The success of my mother's strategy put the three of us at ease with one another at long last.

Years later, I was to hear my mother complain to me that I was getting nowhere as a writer, since by that time I had only published one volume of poems. Why did I not write the sort of thing that made Eddie Cantor, the comedian, rich and famous, she would argue on those occasions when I would visit her and my father. My usual retort would be that Al Capone, the then notorious gangster, was even more famous and rich than Eddie Cantor. I was deeply hurt that she had, as it seemed, reversed herself toward me. I viewed it, to mollify myself, as the result of her advancing age and, as I had to admit to myself, of her real worry about my ability to survive in a competitive world that counted money as the criterion for success and fame. She still cared about me, but her values had somehow gone astray, as it seemed to me, under the influence of my father, who had by that time begun to make a good living for them both as the proprietor of a well-run, prosperous bindery. He had succeeded on his terms. His struggle had paid off.

Several years earlier, when I was about to publish this same book of poems at my own expense but was short of the money I needed, I approached my father in his cubbyhole of an office. He was already assured of a good income from his bindery and was pleased with himself that he could afford a new car and an even fancier house than the red-brick one to which he had moved years before from the cold-water apartment house in the working-class neighborhood. He greeted me pleasantly in his office, which I had not entered since having left for my job with the WPA. We talked awhile about neutral things, and then I spoke of the impending publication of my first book of poems, for which I needed a small sum to complete payment. On my subsistence salary on WPA, I could not spare that small sum. He silently thought about my request, then drew out his checkbook from a desk drawer and wrote out a check, handing it to me with a smile. I read the earlier past into that smile. He was once more happy to hear me speak of my ambition.

He would keep a copy of the book on his desk and, when customers came to discuss their orders with him and saw the book lying face up, he would tell them it was his son's first book. He was proud of it, as he handed it over to them to look through. Nonetheless, as if to guard himself against sentimentality and over-optimism, he would add, "Of course, nothing will come of it. Let him enjoy himself while he can. Life will sink into him one day, and he will change." I don't think he ever quite believed it himself. From the day he received the book from my hands, he treated me with distant respect, as perhaps he would have treated his favorite Russian authors if he had met any of them. And so, for me, the circle had come full turn. We were, in a way, back to where we had started out in our relationship, but the roles were reversed, and I could feel myself vindicated in his eyes and in my own self-image.

A much earlier event also bears upon this episode with my father. One morning as I was having breakfast, being served by my mother, I burst out in despair that I was leaving home forever. I was going to join other boys downtown in Brooklyn to travel by freight car across country. My life in the shop had become too horrible to endure any longer. I had in my pocket exactly twenty cents, not yet having received my allowance for the day from my mother. Without waiting for her to reply or to appeal to me to change my mind, thinking at the same time that I was making quite an effective demonstration of my despair, I ran down the flight of stairs to the street door, my mother calling after me in an agitated voice, and headed for the subway where I was going to catch a train to the Brooklyn Civic Center. There, I had read in the newspaper, boys without jobs, homeless boys, gathered to form groups for mutual protection before searching out freight cars in railroad yards on which to ride across country in search of jobs or, finding none, at least to get away from a sordid life of unemployment and poor food. We were then deep into the Depression. I was going to join the boys and be one of them, finding in them the companionship and understanding I believed I lacked at home. Though I worked and had food, it was nothing to me but the life of an automaton, without a will of my own. My spirit was leaving me, and my misery was mounting.

I spent the first five of my twenty cents for carfare, and I already had begun to worry. I hadn't eaten much breakfast in my turmoil at the table. Hungry, I bought myself a package of salted peanuts for another five cents. Also, I remembered having read in the newspaper that these boys at the Civic Center were the poorest of the poor, their clothes ragged, their hands and faces unclean for lack of soap. They were roughspoken and often hostile and aggressive. I was not too happy about that and, in the meanwhile, I knew I had left my mother in a state of near panic and hysteria. She had clutched her mouth in horror as I fled down the stairs to the street. I could imagine her calling up my father in anguish to say I was gone from them forever. I must say it gave me some satisfaction, despite my feelings of guilt and commiseration with her, that both my parents were probably experiencing a deep anguish at having mistreated me all those years I had been forced to work at the bindery.

When, finally, I arrived within view of the Civic Center, my heart excited, my thoughts filled with the wonder of an unknown adventure, I saw several boys standing at the fountain. They were rough looking, and their faces were grim. They were turning their heads slowly from side to side, as if looking for prey. I grew scared. I stood at a distance and studied the situation for myself as calmly and objectively as I could. I knew that whatever decision I was to make would be a fateful one that would shape my life forever, and it could be at the risk of my life also. I was thinking of these boys, of being in their company. I saw them hunched up like prize fighters, their shoulders slouched forward, about to deliver a blow. I now knew I had had illusions about their having come from my kind of upbringing and interests. Already I had spent my last ten cents on two more bags of peanuts, and I was still hungry, perhaps from anxiety. I was completely broke, without a cent, not even with carfare to take me back to my father's shop. I was already thinking in those terms. But there in the distance stood the Brooklyn Bridge. The bindery was only a mile or so from the bridge on the Manhattan side.

To be able to make myself leave the Civic Center and those boys, I had to admit to myself that I had made a mistake, a willful mistake. I had to write. I had to prove myself a writer. That was my one and overriding goal. Without writing, my life with these boys, even if I survived among them, would be a failure. I turned toward the bridge with a peculiar sense of relief and yet a pride in myself at being able to accept the reality of my circumstance. It would mean hard work and long hours, but I would write. Walking across the bridge, I imagined what the first reaction of my father would be, since I was sure he already had heard from my mother of my leaving. In his way he was probably consumed with worry about me in an awakened, or more likely sharpened, sense of guilt toward me. I would walk in calmly and silently, as if nothing unusual had happened, so that things could go on as they had in the past, as if mechanically, without fuss. As I opened the door to the bindery, my father, his back to the door and facing the street window where the work tables were lined up, turned at the creaking of the hinges and saw me. A broad smile came upon his face, obviously of relief and pleasure but also with a trace of satisfaction. I had returned, as perhaps he had assured my mother and had himself expected.

I was hoping that he would not make a big scene at my return. I yet needed my self-respect so that I could continue to concentrate on the reality that was before me and that I had decided to accept as my life from then on, until I had made a new reality for myself. He went directly to the phone and spoke with my mother in a voice of assurance and satisfaction. I tried to ignore it, and when he got off the phone I was prepared in a businesslike way to return to my job, as he was prepared, and without further ado assigned me to the folding machine at which I was supposed to have been working until then.

My two sisters, Tillie, the older, and Fay, the younger, both attending school, had become a kind of obstacle to my writing. The door to my room opened onto the living room, with its radio and record player, which my sisters enjoyed playing in the evening after having completed their homework. It enraged me when they turned on either set, all in the midst of my trying to write at my "desk," my mother's sewing machine. I would lunge out of my room and turn off the set. They'd run back to my parents in the kitchen, frightened at my action and loudly complaining. Neither of my parents knew what to do in a dilemma between the conflicting claims of their children. Occasionally, my mother would come into the living room and plead with me to let them turn on the set for a short time. Most often I'd refuse in anger. At other times, infrequently, I'd turn my back in silence and withdraw into my room, shutting the door behind me grimly. My two sisters would turn on the set timidly, whispering between themselves, still intimidated by my anger, but would turn it off shortly and return to the kitchen, crying. Those incidents eventually had a negative effect upon our relationship. The three of us were in a situation that had no good solution for any one of us, given the circumstances in which we lived. I felt its tragic implication for us all, but had no choice as a writer madly committed to my craft and to the freedom I needed to practice it, at last to be rid of enslavement to factory work and schedules. Yet there was no denying I cared for both my sisters then and enjoyed their company at other times when we could be at ease with each other, though we found ourselves in adult years in bitter controversy.

My career on the WPA newspaper was ended for me by the Japanese attack on Pearl Harbor. I worked for two years as a handyman in the Kearney, New Jersey, shipyards until I was exempted from the Army and then took a job as admitting officer at Beth Israel Hospital in my neighborhood. It was a 4 to 12 midnight shift, which gave me late morning and early afternoon hours to read and write.

Years later, when I returned to the bindery—mainly at my mother's pleading, my father beginning to age—his sudden collapse from a stroke left the conduct of the business to my brother-in-law, the chief mechanic, and to me, the company salesman and administrator. (My two sisters already were married and with children. I, too, was married and with a son.) The relationship between my brother-in-law and me had been strained since my return to the shop. I had tried to come to terms with him for what he thought was my unfair advantage over him in the business. I was the one who could walk out of the bindery, in his opinion, ostensibly to visit customers, new and prospective. He had a vision of me seated in a library reading and writing. Though I actually did in time introduce new accounts, there was little I could do to disabuse him of his fixed belief. He persisted in criticizing me to my face and in front of the working personnel and to my parents, in particular my father, and especially to my two sisters. I did little or no work of importance to earn my salary in the bindery itself, he charged, and the office work and salesmanship I did were merely a front for evading working at the machines. My father, by this time, had taken a back seat, in a kind of semiretired role, actually in his armchair at one end of the enlarged office, from which he would look on, sometimes in silence, at other times smiling at me sadly.

My brother-in-law, a dropout from school, was hurt that with his ability as an all-around, self-taught mechanic he was not in charge of everything, including me. He needed complete control, including that of the office routine and the selling end, to shore up his image of himself in relationship to me. It bothered him mightily that I would be well dressed in and out of the shop while he could always be found in a mechanic's greasy pants and shirt. I had become in his eyes a leech on the business—my salesmanship, and presumably important administrative work, a front for me to read and write in libraries. In short, he scorned me as an intellectual who lived off the sweat of his physical labor. I was someone to scorn by comparison with his accomplishments, and it seemed to soothe his pride to talk about it in the shop.

With my father's collapse, my brother-in-law began to court one customer in particular, one who happened to be a close neighbor in his town. Together they formed a scheme whereby my brother-in-law would open his own bindery in the building where this customer had his printing plant. Not very long after, the two went into action. My brother-in-law informed me quite calmly one morning before business hours were to begin that he was about to open his own shop and take with him this particular customer, and several others, all of whom were the bread and butter of the business. He had persuaded them that I was not competent to do their work. He pointed out that my interest in writing was more important to me than the bindery, and he convinced them that I would be out of business just as soon as he left to open his own shop. The majority of these accounts had been brought into the bindery through my efforts as a salesman, yet he felt very secure in his actions. In addition to winning over these accounts, he also would legally become a full partner with me in the old business upon my father's death, as it was written in the will my father had signed a year before his collapse. It meant that on my father's death my brother-in-law would be entitled to draw a salary from the very business he was abandoning, at the same time he would be prospering in his own. Neither of my sisters intervened in this sinister scheme. In fact, they approved of it because they sided with my brother-in-law's version of my work in the shop, and they helped it along by remaining silent.

When the scheme did finally come out in the open, leaving me financially devastated, the younger of my two sisters, the one with whom I thought I had felt some personal relationship, refused to help or in any way work to ameliorate the damage I was sure to suffer. To my plea for help and to my wife's plea, she retorted that

it was none of her affair and, anyway, she went on, she was look-
ing out for her own interests. It occurred to me that this could be
the culmination of a long-held unconscious antagonism toward me
arising out of my past conduct toward her and her older sister
when we were living together in our parents' home, I in my room
outside the living room, with its radio and record player. Besides,
as I had already begun to sense, they resented the favored position
my father had made for me by allowing me to leave for home
much before the workday was over so that I would have time to
write in early afternoon when my energies were at their peak. We
have since had no contact, other than a rare plea by my younger
sister to come together again. She, like the other members of the
family, considers herself to be the injured one. I do not these days
see in the telephone directory any evidence that my brother-in-law's
business still exists.

My relations with relatives outside the immediate family are
not very good either. My cousins, male and female, look upon me
(or did in the past; perhaps they have since changed) as someone
odd in wanting to become a writer. The one exception was my
cousin, Edward, who took my ambition seriously. At the time I did
not think I was going to become a full-time poet. My goal then
was to write short stories, the kind that were published in the
Saturday Evening Post, a popular middle-brow magazine of those
years. It was all with the intention of taking my parents, my two
sisters, and myself out of this perpetual struggle to be free of the
cares of money. I had just graduated from high school and looked
toward becoming a huge success as a short-story writer. I had, it
seemed to me then, all the ideas needed to become a success of
the kind the *Saturday Evening Post* approved of. But my short
stories came back with printed, unsigned rejection slips. Something
was wrong, and it had to be with me.

In the meanwhile, my anger and despair at being forced into
my father's employ made a poet of me, as I look back upon it
now—one who had to write fiercely and bitterly of his life and of
the lives of most people, so much like mine, on a treadmill of

working, eating, sleeping, and eventual dying. If my stories with these themes were not going to be accepted, then my poetry, in its truth to life, which I could write for my own sanity and pleasure, would do. It was the truth I wanted to write, for I had once read that "You shall know the truth and the truth shall set you free." If I could not physically free myself of enslavement, I could proclaim its horrors for the world to know, and free myself of the guilt of silence and submission.

Edward understood and was encouraging in his quiet way. He came from a deeply financially and emotionally depressed family, without the means to gain an education. His father, like mine, had been an immigrant from Russia, with no skills at all, and so had brought up his children in hopeless poverty. Ed, though depressed, took a serious, objective view of his situation and tried to understand, talking about it and discussing related books with me that he had read. He made this effort to overcome his sense of foredoomed failure, or at the very least, to seek to discover the meaning of it all from which he could wrest some control through knowledge and, if not entire control, at least enough relief from his depression and from his poor self-image. I did not like to meet him too often. Though my own family, at that time, was not far removed from abject poverty, still I could sense in myself the determination to live beyond it and succeed in my ambition, for the truth had to be told—written out—as my one satisfaction. In Ed, I felt defeat. He was preparing himself for compromise, as I began to sense in his discussions with me. He was planning to go into business with his older brother and, as he said, that would be the end of his reading and thinking. He would prefer it that way because reading and thinking brought him little but depression through his insight into a life already a failure. In business, he could forget failure and live, simply live and do whatever came to hand. It depressed me to hear this, and so gradually, with diplomatic excuses, I discouraged our meetings. He was so typical of many of the young men of my age I knew in my circumstances, and I was not going to allow myself to become another of that kind. I was especially intent about breaking with Edward after having received my invitation to join the WPA Writers Project. In speech, looks, dress, and slump of shoulders, Ed had the appearance to me of death. Sometimes, seated beside him, I thought I could smell it on him.

There was also my friend Bill, who lived around the corner from me at the time I was attending high school. He loved to put out a street newsletter each week. He would type it up in his house on an 8½-by-11 sheet of paper that he would fold to make four pages. Each page would have a different subject, the opening page dealing with games we had played that past week—stoopball especially. Stoopball was played by striking a ball against the edge of a step leading up to the landing at the house door. The ball would sail across the street, and it had to be caught before it bounced in order to "get out" the hitter of the opposing team. Each bounce would count for a base earned, and a ball caught after four bounces meant the hitter had earned a home run. Bill had formed us into teams, which we enjoyed immensely, and so he had much to write about: our successes and failures at bat or at catching, with occasional good-natured ribbings of particular players who had not done so well. At other times Bill would go all out in praise of a certain player who had proved himself sensationally as hitter or catcher. The inside of the front page would deal with the actual professional teams written about in the newspapers. He would give scores and opinions as to which team was likely to win the national championship. The third page dealt with the gossip of the block: who had met a girl recently and liked her and who had gone to a party without inviting his street friends, and so forth. The fourth and last page was given over to so-called creative writing, from jingles to serious poems, in rhyme and in free form. This was the page I would contribute to regularly, early evidence of my public acceptance as a writer. I was infinitely grateful to Bill, and we became good friends. I was invited to his house during the Christmas holidays and was offered the cookies and cakes and drinks his mother had prepared for the celebration.

Bill was sad to see me leave the neighborhood forever one day as I was escorting my bride-to-be to our prospective apartment in Manhattan. He tried to keep in touch with me by mailing me a New Year's card each year for many years from Baltimore, and I would promise myself to visit him and, as often, urge him to visit me. Never, though, did he write back. It was a strange relationship. I would write, and he would not reply. Had he been hurt that I had married, as if having given up all the promise I had meant to him as a writer? Did he ever marry? When the New Year cards stopped coming, I knew he was dead. I think of these comments on our relationship as a memorial to him, the very first person outside my family to have recognized me as a writer.

2. Living with Change

Early in the forties, feeling desperate about my lack of literary success, feeling totally unworthy of the title "poet"—in fact, feeling unworthy as a man and participant in the world because of my continued failure to be recognized as a poet—I fell in love with a beautiful black woman who was then working with me in my father's bindery. The love lifted me out of my self-pity. I knew well enough of what my love consisted, but here was a black woman who, though beautiful and young, was already condemned to a life of drudgery as an unskilled laborer in a factory, never to emerge from it into the light of pleasure and self-regard. We had a fate in common, I then believed, but I had something else, which made me happy, yet with a sense of guilt about myself: I was able in my paltry position as my father's assistant in the shop to attract a woman who, like me, was looking for a life that would lift her out of her misery. In short, we saw in each other the means with which to relieve unhappiness with ourselves, she through attaching herself to the son of the boss, and I through acquiring a lovely mistress as a symbol of my power. The color difference between us did not matter to either of us; we both were suffering from a loss of status in our own eyes. We both were among the outcasts of society and had found a way to enhance each other's image by falling in love. If this sounds crude and self-serving by each of us, it is, but that it was intentionally so was not the fact. We were acting out of a deep need that was not in our control. We were acting out a compulsion that demanded to be fulfilled within the very society that had shaped us.

Of course, I see all this in hindsight; yet at the time, I was conscious of my feelings toward myself as I looked out on the world of literary recognition from which I was excluded, just as she felt herself excluded from the world of material wealth and status. I speak of all this openly because it represents my first experience with a black person and has remained for me the touchstone of my future experiences. Eventually, she became acutely self-conscious of her blackness in relation to me, as we began to find it more and more difficult to keep our relationship secret. Secret it had to be, we thought, if she were not to be fired by my father, who we felt would not tolerate such a relationship in the shop should it become known. Besides, there were other men in his shop who would take it as a signal to make their own advances to her—I, the boss's son, having shown the way. Because she was black, their thinking would go, she was vulnerable in her inferior social position to the power and blandishments of the whites. Finally, when our relationship became obvious, the predictable followed quickly, and my father, rather than firing us both, also became involved in reaching for her out of some secret envy of and competitiveness with me in the world of business. He was the one who had the final and absolute power over everyone, including me, to do with as he wished in the workings of the bindery—a power, apparently, that did not exclude attempting to seduce a woman in his employ through the threat of losing favor in his eyes, no matter how gently put, and so, inferentially, making her feel unwelcome in the shop if he were refused. She resisted and was apprehensive about keeping her job. I too became nervous in his presence, since I too depended on him for my livelihood. Later in life, as my experiences in the business world grew, I came to realize that he was typical of such men in power.

We were then living through the last lingering effects of the Great Depression. And so, in the slim hope of retrieving the original secrecy between Sara and me, I began to assume an impersonal manner toward her and tried to keep a distance between us as we worked. To the men, it was a signal that I had abandoned her to them. My father, when she happened to arrive earlier than usual for work, would be alone in the shop waiting for just such an opportunity to press himself upon her. She understood it all. She saw herself as being placed by me in the role of a sacrifice, an offering to their power, and so when I approached her with orders for a particular job, she would deliberately banter about us in front of the others to embarrass me as she was being embarrassed and humiliated too. And she would turn scornfully to flirt with the other men, as I stood there, to show that she knew what was happening and meant to defy it. One morning, before entering the shop for work, she confronted me in the corridor to accuse me bitterly of having used her as a convenience like any white man would and then dumping her. The next morning she was gone.

My guilt toward her was deep. I had no excuse but my own cowardice. To continue to associate myself with her in the open against the wishes and rivalry of my father; to bind myself with her in exile from society as I knew it then, with both of us fired and with no jobs; to have my need to write frustrated by desperate poverty; to find myself with her and her people, abused, insulted, trampled on, ignored, and forgotten, as they were in their sufferings; to be, in effect, obliterated from society—all this I could not take and did not dare risk. Frightened and repelled, I suddenly awakened to the significance of my attachment to her, and was profoundly sad at being unable to face the consequence of my attachment. Many years had to go by before I could come to terms with myself, years in which I finally knew that never again would I let myself be drawn into such cowardly behavior toward anyone. With this sorely gained knowledge of myself, I could become reconciled to my wish to live well and write my poems as a balance to my deep, pervasive sense of defeat and self-hatred. Time and events were to test my resolve to remain steadfast in a crisis, and that test would come about in an unexpected and, again, a frightening way.

As my reputation grew among poets, critics, and readers, I received invitations to tour colleges to teach and read from my poems, until one day I settled upon a permanent position at York College of the City University of New York. At my father's death in the early sixties, after I had bought out my brother-in-law, I sold everything of value in the shop—machinery and tools—to pay off the debts incurred by my father's long illness. I gave up all business contacts and accounts, leaving myself with only a week's salary to start on the adventure of my life as a poet. York College in the late sixties was planned as an institute of innovative programs and teaching, and I was delighted to be chosen, not only for the position of poet-in-residence, but also as a teacher. It was going to be a life exactly the opposite, emotionally and intellectually, of what I had led for years in the family business.

In the meantime, I had taken an apartment in a building just around the corner from the school in order to avoid traveling twice and sometimes three times a week from home on the East End of Long Island, a distance of more than one hundred miles. I was renting an apartment at the recommendation of one of the secretaries in our school and settled in; however, she, without telling me in advance, was leaving to take an apartment out of the area where, she finally confided, she would feel much safer than in Jamaica. The school had only recently moved from predominantly white Bayside to South Jamaica, one of the concentrations of black population in Queens County. The student body was reflecting the change, a shift I had not noticed until she had conveyed to me her decision to move.

Her decision alarmed me. Had I placed myself in a dangerous position? From various neighbors in the building I had gotten reports of handbag snatching in the very courtyard of the building and of apartments broken into and vending machines in the laundry room smashed open for their coins. These incidents and others, I was told, were all the work of men and women of the immediate area. The police took notes, looked over the damage or inspected the loss, and left silently. With such reports, reinforced by the departure of the secretary from the building and the area, what was I to think? I felt again that old fear that had its roots in my relationship to Sara. This time I was in her world where it could do as it wished, and in its wrath could force me to live in that abject fear and humiliation that had been its lot for so many years among the whites. I sensed my past had caught up with me; my life had come full circle with a vengeance, and this time there was no escape.

New York was the place where I chose to earn my living, where I wished to stay. I could, if I wished, accept a position in a school elsewhere. I had turned down Berkeley and Wisconsin, each having invited me. New York was my home. I had been raised here. All its streets, avenues, its people, its speech were as familiar to me as my own features and, in a manner of speaking, my own features—emotional, intellectual, and creative—were made up of those with which I was familiar and had grown with in New York. I had tried teaching in schools out of town, only to find myself missing the sounds, the movements, the variety of life and events, and the intellectual ferment of New York. I missed it all, as I had missed my parents at their deaths. In New York I felt at ease with life. There was no leaving New York for me. I would have to work out my destiny as a poet and man here among the sights and people with whom I had grown up, and that included the people of Sara of my father's shop. I still had not forgotten my grief.

But I had to face my fears. There were many young black men at school from the South Jamaica area, as one result of our college's move. These youths carried themselves aggressively, as if deliberately defying what they were being taught. Their behavior seemed to be a show of anger; for all the years of exclusion from the mainstream of American life, they intended to avenge themselves in the very citadel of American aspiration by converting it into the image of their own lives. A civil war seemed to be in the making. The time was the mid-sixties, and these black youths were on the crest of the student rebellions that were overwhelming schools throughout the country. They were taking over the very halls of the university from which, formerly, they had been shut out.

In anguish as to how to deal with them personally, dangerous as they appeared to me and to the functioning of the school, I thought back to my relationship with Charley Johnson, who had worked under my supervision in my father's shop. Charley, a black, had been our principal mechanic for one section of the shop. He and I had struck up a guarded camaraderie, guarded as it would have to be between boss and worker. By that time, Sara had been gone for several years. We had to refuse Charley his justified raise to his requested union scale, and one day he quit, without giving notice. Some months later, as I was walking through the corridor of a huge printing plant on the way to its main office to solicit bindery business, who should I see emerging from a side door of the plant but Charley, apparently on the way to the john. He recognized me at once; I was in a kind of absorbed state about the business prospects ahead of me. With a shout of joy and surprise, Charley came charging toward me, embracing me by the shoulders and grinning into my startled face with a wondrous, excited look that I had gotten to know him by, and that stamped him for me as Charley. At first, staggered by his flying embrace, shocked out of my absorption to find him in front of me, I was overwhelmed, finding it hard to speak, to discover that he still thought of me with affection.

We earned our profit solely from cheap labor, and it had to be cheap for us to stay in business. We were nonunion and had to compete with union shops. The workers we drew on came mainly from among the poor, uneducated blacks, all of whom had been excluded from training for the better jobs, which the union that controlled the jobs withheld by excluding blacks from membership. So these poor blacks came to us to accept what we could offer—training in the rudiments of elementary routines that they would work at for the rest of their stay with us, with barely a raise beyond a dollar or two each year in recognition of their reliability.

But Charley was not silent and accepting. Before coming to us, he had managed to bluff and bluster his way into better jobs in nonunion shops and, through a succession of skilled jobs from which he had been fired after revealing himself to be incompetent, he had learned enough to do a little better at each succeeding one. Eventually, by the time he came to us, he was at least familiar with his trade, though with much yet to learn. The tension between us became high, as he felt himself threatened once again with firing, and sometimes his language would turn threatening too, as if he were defending his very life, but we kept him on because it was difficult, if not impossible, to find a white man for the wages we were paying him. In the meantime, however, growing more skilled on the job, he began to grasp many of its details and to relax and even invite conversation. And so we counted on his staying on and, because of his newly found sense of belonging, were planning to increase his salary, though still needing to keep it below the union scale. But we had not counted on his native drive and temperament, his restlessness to improve himself, and his wonderful swagger—so sure of himself. A week before he had stopped working for us we had had a muted but tense discussion in the office where he justifiably demanded a further increase in salary corresponding to his increasing efficiency. I had to turn him down. During his last months, he and I had broken through the usual worker-employer tension to a relationship in which we came to recognize and accept each other as individuals. Working together every day over difficult problems during his training period, we had grown to understand each other's language and point of view, which led to a corresponding mutual respect and exchange of confidences that reflected our understanding and mutual acceptance. It was a relationship that both of us were happy with, and so the talk between us concerning his deserved raise was difficult for us both, with grimaces of pain and long stretches of silence, at last causing us to part with a foreboding of what was to follow.

And now I was meeting him in the corridor of his new and obviously better-paying position in a much larger nonunion shop. He had made it on his own again. As we stood together, I was grateful to him for remembering me with so much affection as to embrace me warmly. Both of us talked excitedly and suddenly he grabbed me by the shoulders again. It was the old Charley in high spirits. After hasty exchanges of news and promises between us to meet again somehow, we went our separate ways, but not before he had managed to tell me quickly about his new job, about how much more it paid than what I had been able to offer. He spoke with no show of bitterness toward me. He was simply filled with joy and pride in himself.

And so, to him, I had not simply been the manager of exploited labor. I was still the one with whom he had shared confidences. This meeting in the corridor became a turning point in my own self-regard as man and poet, depressed as I had been in my key role in an exploitative industry.

And so, as I sat in my office at college remembering Charley, I knew I could and would find a way to reach the students there. Their sense of me was identical with what Charley had originally brought into the shop. Besides, it was a challenge to be accepted on my own terms, as it had been to him to be accepted on his terms. We had formed a relationship that no economic necessity alone could have brought about. But the great difference between the past and the present was that I had nothing to withhold from my students, as I had had to from Charley. I had everything to offer now.

I was nevertheless troubled by one student in particular. Tall and broad-shouldered like Charley, he was less high-spirited and jovial. A student in my remedial class in English, he represented in acute, angry form all the others who came and went as they pleased, sometimes showing up in class, however late, and then sauntering out in the middle of the writing exercise, and sometimes not even bothering to attend class for a whole week. Mostly, they came from families in which mothers and fathers toiled at manual labor to come home exhausted, too angry and despairing of their lives to oversee or wish to oversee the education of their children, for whom they felt the same hopelessness as for themselves. They were of the same circumstances as those we had employed in my father's shop. Given their conditions, they could feel no hope for their futures, much less those of their children, and so this attitude had conveyed itself to the children who, like their parents, kept their anger within, expressing it only in their desultory manner inside and outside the classroom. To receive repeated failing grades meant to them only that they could expect nothing else from a white teacher. It was what they had been led to expect at the hands of white persons in power and so, except for this one student among them, they preferred to ignore those failing grades.

But that student, openly and scornfully, demanded an explanation for his grades. He would stride up to my desk to point out on the paper that there was nothing wrong with a particular sentence. He had meant to use the right tense but inadvertently had written the wrong one, and so was entitled to a passing grade. He argued loudly for the benefit of everyone else in class, and his voice would rise to a threatening climax, which I considered as nothing less than a threat to my person. The other students would look on in silence, amused and grinning, watching the powerfully built youth tower above me, trying to bully me into revising his grade. Scenes such as this were to repeat themselves after every grading of homework or class exam. In the silence in which I would sit, emotionally exhausted, the youth would return to his seat, swaggering through his defeat, feeling himself compensated. He was like Charley at his worst, except that Charley would have quickly shifted from this threatening manner, recognizing the danger in it, that is, in getting himself fired. At school, however, no one could be fired, especially not for talking loudly. We had an open-admissions policy, and we were accepting students as they were, not as we expected them to be. Nevertheless, through my fear, I could perceive his fear deep beneath his threatening tone. Like Charley, he did not relish the prospect of failing, and it was worrying him. However, it was only weeks later in the quiet of my apartment, after the first shock of his behavior had passed, that I could make the connection between him and Charley.

In class, after a few moments of silence in which I would find the strength to go on, I would raise my head to look at the two exceptions among the students, two I had already at the start of the term singled out as earnest and hardworking, one a girl, the other a young man, both quiet and with a ready smile for the others, but without a real camaraderie with them. At the end of the period, the two would walk out of the room separately and unaccompanied. Along with the bullying youth and the others, all came from the same poor neighborhoods, as their registration records revealed to me.

One day, as I gathered myself together again, I called on the girl to read aloud from her paper, and the class proceeded to settle down in silence to listen. She received my oral comments with nods and quickly offered to rewrite the paper, an offer I accepted. As she spoke, I suddenly became aware that the others in class, including the bullying youth, were gazing at her almost with jealousy. I was moved. They appeared so helpless at that moment. How, I asked myself, was I going to bridge the gap between myself and these youths who yearned to know but were trapped in their hostilities, their angers and hatreds, all directed at me as surrogate for the repressive forces in their lives? What did I need to do to help them? I was born of a family of Jewish immigrants who had come from Russia, where they had been bitterly persecuted, and who had not had an opportunity in this country to study the English language because they were forced to work twelve to fourteen hours a day, six days a week, simply to survive. They had spoken to one another in Yiddish, the pervasive language in the home, and inevitably, I had come to absorb the Yiddish idiom and as a student in class would write the kind of English that directly transcribed Yiddish turns of phrases. My speech too was affected. Often it had been brought to my attention, satirically, by student friends from second- and third-generation families who knew better and by teachers who encircled the strange-sounding phrases on my assignment papers and in the margins scribbled critical remarks, sometimes overtly hostile. My self-consciousness about my speech and writing had made me, too, defensive, sometimes angry. I was not comfortable with myself, or at such times with others. I came to feel that it was a testing time for my determination to overcome my problems. In the meantime, I could observe my parents struggling simply to keep afloat. They were never to rise to a position in life where they could be accepted, but were often laughed at, my father especially, for mispronouncing words in his business relationships and sometimes creating new bizarre-sounding words and phrases out of his ignorance and his bold eagerness to succeed.

I would think these thoughts in my office and in my apartment as I would sit grading student papers during the week. Eventually, particularly during the Second World War when his business was booming, my father was able to pay off the mortgage on his house and purchase a new car, for him a sign of his acceptance and respectability in the community, though there was really no community for him beyond his family of brothers and sisters, in his same circumstances, and from them he obtained that acceptance and respectability. Nevertheless, he remained the hardest worker in his shop, conditioned by his earliest struggles. He would arrive in the shop just after dawn and stay at work late into the night, long after everyone else had gone home, working at his machines to earn that extra profit that afforded him his new car and house free of mortgages.

I always understood my father's obsession with security, as it expressed itself in his drive to work to keep his shop afloat. It was his pride, and it was a pride of ownership and mastery too, signifying the security of his person and his identity and those of his immediate family. It was his particular distinction in his competitive field. His customers admired him. Yet, I could not go along with him on that basis, since his use of cheap, nonunion labor was at the root of his success. I could not sympathize. In his obsession with his position in the world of the bindery, he had become arrogant and blind toward others. As an exile in this country, he had been an awkward, floundering immigrant, exploited by those above him in power, especially by the printers who controlled bindery jobs that, withheld at crucial times, could have bankrupted him and sent him and the family to the welfare lines. He had to accept their prices forced on him. By working from dawn until past dinnertime, he managed at least to break even, and keep the shop in existence, but that was all. The Great Depression had traumatized him.

I used to share these thoughts and other remembrances of the past with Charley in the privacy of my office when he would wander in during lunchtime to sit down and chat with me about his problems of keeping an apartment and family together. His record player, which he brought in for entertainment during lunch hour, would be blaring out his favorite jazz tunes while we talked of our backgrounds, our upbringing, our responsibilities. As I thought back, I saw in those episodes with Charley the solution to my problem with that unhappy, explosive young man in class, and with the others too, but I decided to concentrate only on him, as the key to the solution. Everything else would follow easily if I could ease the conflict with this student. I knew I did not need to develop any special technique of teaching to bring about the miracle of standard grammar in my students. In a university dedicated to the open-admissions policy and swamped by the illiteracy of its students, no such miracle existed anywhere, but it was my first duty to get the student to feel that I understood, wished the best for him, and would work with him to the utmost of my abilities, for as a person he was my peer. I would make that feeling clear to him to help rid him of his fears, but in turn he would have to treat me as a person so that I could help him.

In a few weeks, after persuading him to stay after class, I was able to induce him to visit me at my office where we could discuss more at length and in detail those differences between us. At first, our discussions focused on problems with English, particularly his ambivalence about learning to use it effectively. He was not stupid by any standard. He understood himself well, especially in relation to the English language, which he saw as the instrument of white power whereby he would be made even more subservient by adopting the language of white power and all it stood for. We talked about these feelings.

It was not as if he was unalterably opposed to learning what I had to teach but that he needed to be reassured that learning it would actually give him the tool with which to better his condition. He could manage it, we concluded, with the very means that he feared meant his continued subjugation. He could manage it by his strength of will, backed by strength of purpose and appreciation of the paradox of learning what he had to learn. He had no difficulty in grasping these insights, but because of the differences of our use of language, it took us some time to arrive at a formulation both of us could accept. In the process, we became at ease with each other, observing and gaining confidence from the effort we saw each was putting into the process. Much of his life-style came to the surface, and this life-style, as we both recognized, was centered on his deep frustrations in an impoverished home life with angry, tired, poorly paid working parents who could give him neither financial nor emotional help, much as my own parents had been too burdened to support me. It was a relief to me to hear him out and respond as I had not been able to do with Charley. The situation here in my office was exactly the opposite of the earlier one. I passionately demanded that this husky young man make a life for himself that he could respect and offered to help him in every possible way both in my office and classroom. At one time, we leaned back in our chairs, amazed at the leap we had made from our first tense confrontations in class to this open, free give-and-take between us. If, in his case, it was because he felt me reaching out to him, it was only because I had no choice but to do it for the sake of us both. Through circumstances, through history, through the nature of human bondage, we were together, in need of one another for our lives' sakes.

But what of my role as poet during all these years and experiences? When I left New York to take a position as visiting lecturer at the University of Kentucky, I was leaving simply for a lark, taking to the hinterlands, and it was not to be for long. Everything outside New York was simply camping ground, as the saying goes in Manhattan. In New York I could spend endless hours seated in coffee houses chatting and discussing with poet friends, then leave to stroll the side streets of brownstones, apartment houses, parks, theatres, restaurants, book shops, antique stores. Even Lower Manhattan fascinated me, with its ancient factory lofts, where I had first learned to sweat at manual labor to earn my pay. Nevertheless, it fascinated me because it was yet so mysterious to me—its swift, ruthless, industrial, and commercial pace, alien to my idealized conception of a city. Much as I wrote of that area's savage, relentless search for gain, its indifference to humans, its power to destroy equally with its power to create, I felt myself belonging to it. I felt I should belong at this center of an American vortex of enterprise and culture.

When I left to teach in Kentucky I promised myself to return. New York was my native ground, and I knew I could not exist as a poet without returning to it to become once more infused with its mad energy, its multiple conflicting interests and issues. New York was for me the world intensified, and I had a seat in its midst from which to watch and join in. I would come back to it with renewed appreciation of its unique character, its strengths, its variety, its marvelous confusions. It was because of my reputation as a poet of the city that I had been invited to the hinterlands to teach the ways of the city, its thinking, its literature, its people. My presence would be the presence of the city itself in the classroom at the university, and I was proud to have been so chosen.

From the University of Kentucky I went on the University of Kansas for a year and then to Vassar, in each school teaching a workshop in the writing of poetry and a survey course in contemporary American poetry. By the time I began at Vassar, I had settled my family on the East End of Long Island. We had given up our New York apartment, finding it much less expensive to live on the Island. And so after three years of living in open territory of trees, meadows, lakes, and mountains in the South (Lexington, Kentucky) and in the Middle West (Lawrence, Kansas), I would continue in the same spaciousness and quiet by living in the countryside on Long Island. I felt a change coming over me. I was learning to relax, to study the trees, the grass, the sky, and the birds, and to write of them with affection and wonder, asking myself how I could have missed it all. Had I simply ignored it while living in Manhattan, even when strolling through a park in the city? For me city life meant being able to concentrate on issues and people. Nature, where it showed itself on the sidewalks and in parks, was merely the background for my intense inner life. I had paid little attention to nature.

But in the Midwest and in the South and in the Far West, where I gave extended readings and workshops, I felt myself becoming a different being, open to senses that I had not thought existed in me, open to sights and sounds, to hours of solitude amid trees, before meadows and lakes, and in view of snow-covered peaks. After my return to New York, and later in 1968 my appointment at York College, I felt myself back home. Everything else I had seen and lived with outside New York had been beautiful but not my way, for it had all served to make the intellectual excitement, the emotional variety, the vast panoply of diverse lives in New York that much more precious to me.

It was the secretary who had recommended me to the Jamaica apartment, and who had left out of fright to live elsewhere, who brought to consciousness in me a change in New York I had not been fully aware of in my excitement at returning. I began to notice more closely a change in the composition of the population from what I remembered of it before my departure for Kentucky. The year was 1969. In the subway where I had been used to seeing mostly the faces of white men and women, I seemed now to see mostly men and women with black faces, Asiatic faces, and dark Mediterranean complexions. For such a short space of time—four years' absence from New York—the change was baffling. The subways now were full of the loud chatter of Spanish-speaking voices and the drawl of southern voices, all mingled together with the raucous radios of the youths—black and white.

On nearly every ride, I would see men tippling bottles hidden in brown paper bags while leaning drunkenly against the train doors. After a long swig, they would leer defiantly at the passengers. The atmosphere was tense, and the minority of seated whites either would stare straight ahead at their reflections in the windows opposite them or else bury their heads in their newspapers and pretend that they were not present and listening. They were the tense ones in the train. Sometimes a group of young blacks would come charging into the train at a station, stop, and begin staring hostilely at passengers—black and white. They would break into derisive laughter at some joke among themselves or at a comment about the passengers. They enjoyed acting menacing together. The tension in the train would become unbearable, and many passengers stood at the doors and seemed to be getting off at the next stop, if simply to leave these youths behind. New York certainly had become strange to me. I did not feel at home.

My writing in the past about the city had concentrated on other facts and situations—the commercial pace and atmosphere of New York that was so pervasive and dominated the city with indifference to anything that could not satisfy the grasp for gain. I was writing out of my own experience in offices and factories and in the streets, much as I saw my own life resemble those of the vast majority of people in the same circumstances as mine. I had not given much thought to minorities in particular, but now I was teaching in a school that was predominantly black and filled with youths who were from families even more deprived than I had experienced. Many of the youths on the train reminded me of my students in their tough manner and talk. There but for the grace of chance were my students, with brown paper bags wrapped around wine bottles, shouting and gesticulating menacingly in subway trains. They were my new experience in New York.

And what did this new experience have in common with my past? That was the question I had to ask myself in my office while grading student papers, or in my apartment alone in a mostly black neighborhood. I needed to know the answer to that question, and I began to see the answer more clearly through time and experience with these youths in and out of class. I was growing more and more adjusted to the change that earlier in my arrival in New York had been so strange to me and so alienating to my idea of New York.

My answer came to this: If my parents had had to suffer exile in the American society itself, which I too had had to suffer, yet were able eventually to gain a foothold on the mainland, so to speak, how much worse was it for these youths who felt in their very bones an exile that went to the root of being—rejected outright for their humanity as blacks. It was a far more threatening experience than the one my parents and I had had to face. These youths were literally being threatened in their lives by being rejected in their humanity. They were being murdered by being ostracized. Was it any wonder that, feeling in their nerves this calculated rebuff to their claim as humans, they should throw themselves recklessly into self-destructive acts out of despair with their rejected selves?

From time to time, just such a neighborhood youth, waving his bottle overhead, would stagger into the lobby of the school, shouting obscenities and jeering at the guards. Those black students who were present would laugh self-consciously but move off to their classes sadly, while the guards, themselves black, would gently guide the young man out into the street again, closing the door behind him. The white students witnessing the incident would remain silent and attentive until it was over and then leave for their classes too—but silent throughout. Perhaps they were considering leaving the school for another less frightening, as I myself had been. I had no choice but to stay. One doesn't simply sit down and write about changed conditions in one's life, as if they were simply matters for statistics, and expect those changes to come about automatically because of their having been written about. I knew I had not been prepared for such a change as I first witnessed on my return to New York. What I needed was to be able to see these despairing youths as my own people in need of help.

I had begun teaching night classes at the school in order to save my day hours for writing and reading. But teaching at night meant walking home alone through the dark in an area with a high crime rate, one that was well known for drug peddling during the daytime. Each night I had to negotiate the streets by myself to and from classes. I was prepared for injury, robbery, or even death. One night, as I was speaking after class with one of my black students about his writing problems, I discovered that we had to walk the same route on the way home, he to the subway and I to my apartment. We left together and said goodnight to each other at the courtyard of my building, while he continued briskly up the street to the subway entrance around the corner. Eventually, it turned out that several more students, also black, were using the same route on their way home, and we managed each night after class to form a group and walk together, discussing class work and related problems. I was rid of my fears. Youths who were standing on the street corners would look from a distance at one white man surrounded by three or four blacks. It might have looked strange to them, but they must have known we were coming from school. Among ourselves, we grew close enough over the fourteen weeks of the semester to speak candidly with one another. The two black women who walked with us spoke of their relief at being with us. They did not have to say more. The black male student with us, a former navy sailor and a powerfully built man, nodded in approval. The fear was not a matter of blacks against whites. It was the desperate against the more fortunate.

Slowly I came to feel that I was back home in New York again. No, the situation in New York had not changed very much in all this time. The cast of characters had changed, but the theme remained what it had been before my departure for the University of Kansas, only it had grown more intense. I could again distinguish what I and others would have to do, without thought to or consciousness of race or color. What finally mattered was the motive for living, and those of us who wished to make a life for ourselves worthwhile were together as always, as in our small group walking together through the dark street. This was always the way in this city, as we looked out upon the miserable who were often driven to crime, with guarded compassion to help where we could, to make of our own lives such a model that could be accepted by others.

I am back to writing about New York and about myself in it, directly and indirectly. New York is again the source from which

I affirm myself and my neighbors and the whole of the city's multiplex meaning.

Sadly, since writing this essay while living in Jamaica, I have moved back to my family house in East Hampton. One afternoon, while standing in the lobby of my apartment house on 95th Street waiting for the elevator to take me up to my sixth-floor apartment, a young man came swiftly up behind me, threw an arm around my neck, totally immobilizing me, and demanded my money, as he began searching through my pockets with his free hand. To be brief about this horrifying experience, I quietly indicated where my wallet was located, in my breast pocket. He allowed me to remove it, sensing I was not planning to draw a gun. I had managed to keep a slight smile so as to let him know I had no such weapon on me nor planned any violence, but that I wished to get this over with as quickly and peaceably as possible. With my slight smile as a signal between us, he opened the door to the elevator for me to enter. I stepped into it, but not before searching his face for his motive in opening the door for me. Nevertheless, I stepped in with some hope that he had no intention of stepping in with me to do me harm. The elevator door closed behind me, with him looking through the porthole window to watch me as the elevator began its ascent. I was totally traumatized with fear, and I knew I could no longer live in this building or neighborhood if I valued my life and peace of mind. The apartment building entrance was never guarded, and the streets all night were vacant of people, all in their apartments, too frightened to emerge. My students were no longer accompanying me to the door of my building. They had changed to other schedules. The option of moving into another neighborhood in Queens or Manhattan was not mine either. The rents were skyrocketing. Significantly, the rents in Jamaica remained depressed, and so the choice was narrowed down to returning to East Hampton, where my family—wife and daughter—stayed, and where I had a study, but again I would be faced with the problem of driving back and forth to class as often as three days a week. At least I knew that my expenses would be reasonably stabilized. Perhaps I could have asked my present students to accompany me to the door of my Jamaica apartment building, but how was I to know that another young man would not be lurking in the lobby or the courtyard waiting for just such a person as myself to arrive alone in the silent night?

After moving from Jamaica, I switched the courses I was teaching from evening to daytime, sacrificing my leisure time for the sake of safety. Teaching at night had been one of my true pleasures in my relationship with students, most of whom, differing from day students, were working men and women with a strong dedication to improving their lot through education, and we had enjoyed each other for the benefits we were deriving from one another—they the knowledge and know-how I could convey to them, and I the eagerness and sincerity of their ambition. I will miss them, but the issue for me in New York still remains what it has been through the years, that of poverty versus opportunity, with the tragedy that is in it for numberless people who are mired in hatred and self-hatred and self-doubt as poverty sinks into them to poison their well-being and sense of life. I remain the writer who must record this and other facts about New York, not simply for the record, but to make it known, felt, and acted upon before it is too late.

✺ 3. Surrealist Interlude ✺

My first contact with Surrealism goes back as far as the thirties, when the famous magazine, *Transition,* was still publishing. I had met a youth of my age, who was into automatic writing, which he had learned about from studying the issues of *Transition,* with its Surrealist poetry by poets of French, English, and other nationalities. I was intrigued by my new friend's experiments with automatic writing, which he described to me as the process of letting go, letting the mind find its language without interference by the ego, which had been formed by the society in which one lived. In other words, to write automatically, one had to sink beneath the surface of one's customary ways of thought and expression and values to reach that level where we are uniquely ourselves. One had to suspend one's interfering ego from judging and guiding in order to land upon strange new territory, our surprising self. Automatic writing was its other name.

Well, I tried it and found automatic writing for me an impossibility, perhaps because I was so deeply immured in my society. Still, the idea of piercing beneath the surface still appealed to me, and I began to look for a method other than automatic writing. I knew it was the method advocated by the greatest Surrealist poets of the time, Breton among them and the leading theorist, but I had to find my own way. I struck upon the method of arbitrarily starting a poem with an outlandish statement, a statement as far removed from probability as I could devise for myself, and then following through in the "logic" of that statement. Unfortunately for my career as a Surrealist poet, I continued to insist upon making some kind of sense of these outlandish statements, unreal and dreamlike or nightmarish as they seemed even to me. I had to find the clue to their existence, and I also became keenly aware that such wild statements as I was devising for myself had to be coming unquestionably from beneath the surface of my ordinary perceptions. In brief, I was beginning to realize that in my own peculiar way I had reached the level where language was divorced from conventional use and was dealing strictly with dream material. In short, a Surrealist field was there in me to make use of. However, Surrealist writing in its pure sense is not open to meaning, is not written to bring meaning to the reader. Hardly. And so, stubbornly seeking to find meaning in my waking dream at my desk, I found myself still reaching for those Surrealist elements—such as improbability, exaggeration, violent juxtaposition, and outright states of contradiction—but not with the purpose of mystifying or "opening out" to new worlds à la Breton, but for the simple purpose of discovering myself in a kind of wilderness to see what I could make of it, as if to challenge my survival and its worth. There was a fun side to this too—to discover myself as I am, or think I am, beneath the accepted social character I had invented for myself or had been helped by society to invent. I wanted the pleasure of the bizarre, if that was what would result; it would be a pleasurable change from my social self, urbane as I had become. I anticipated and worked toward the grotesque, the weird, and the incredible, no matter what its significance for the interested, alert reader for whom I was creating a meaning out of all these wild inventions. The meaning was mine exclusively and was brought to the writing but for the reader to discover, at least as one of the pleasures of the wild. It was exciting to me that I could find meaning in such images and situations, and I believed I had gone Surrealism one better by actually letting the reader in on the process to discover a personal meaning beneath his or her own surface, making of the reader and the writer partners beneath the skin.

4. Your Child as Writer

To become a writer is to enter a highly precarious occupation—as you look back upon your own experience, crowded with crises that are financial, emotional, and domestic. All sorts of problems arise when you discover to your astonishment and distress that you need to make a living and find companionship in your struggle.

Loneliness is the most difficult hazard to overcome in writing. You are mostly away from relationships that are precious to you. You are in isolation when it's people you need, people to whom you can appeal for help in your thinking and in bridging the time between bouts of writing. That is because you haven't written enough or received the acceptances that give you the confidence with which to withstand the loneliness. You too often present a sour or grim demeanor in the house, hardly conducive to the peace and pleasure that should emanate from a marriage. When your own child elects to become a writer it sets up tremors in your warning system, the way the Richter scale works in an earthquake. You want to know where the damage will be most severe to the child. I feared for my daughter's well-being, and yet at the same time I experienced the thrill beneath my shock that she had in her the excitement of search for meaning in language, and I felt a tremor of warning that she was going to risk her most concentrated thinking on paper to discover for herself whether she came up to her own standards of excellence. It was going to be a test of worth in her own eyes, and I was deeply gratified that I had a child who could attempt with all seriousness such a hazardous undertaking, the search for one's inimitable self and one's connection with the world. Here in the family was a writer like myself. She was about to join with me and leave to the future the hazards of finances, emotional insecurity, and relationships, in her intense need to become.

I was to learn her decision when she was in her early teens through her proud mother. I could gather from the poems she showed me at my urging (she shied away from approaching me directly) that she was committed. I noticed at once that her poems were by no means imitations of my own. The intensity of her imagery and rhythms were unquestionably arising from a place with which I could sense no direct affinity. It was emotional and concentrated on things that would not have occurred to me.

I have since occasionally offered to help edit her poems and her fiction—but only as I learned of her troubled comments about being recognized and accepted as a writer in her own identity, independently of being my daughter. In the poems I could see she had nothing to fear in that respect. We were not writing in the same stream of thought or feeling. That was plain. Still, it was also apparent to me that she was, unique to her relationship to me, beginning to undergo the problems of that relationship as one burden she would have to carry as poet. There was no way around it. Meeting it head-on was the only solution.

The publication of her first volume of poems, *The Flaw,* established her independently of me in style and in person publicly. Though the struggle remains, it has become less a burden, as I sense it, and more a challenge, a given from which to work out her own destiny as poet.

I am more proud of her than I can say and as a poet I feel somehow strengthened in my work and being because of her presence in the same field with me.

5. All Good Writing Is Teaching

My own tradition as teacher and writer is rooted in personally identifying with the subject under study. This is not to deny the efficacy of study through objective means, where they are available. But, thereafter, I am ready to offer, to the best of my judgment, my own responses and to declare them personal and interpretive. With this method to guide me, I am always ready to encourage a student in expression of personal relationship to the subject, even when the student has no basis for a considered opinion.

It seems to me that such an approach is organic to study in the humanities, especially in literature, which is, if nothing else, the product of intensely personal interpretation and presentation at its best. To offer a student less than this freedom in his or her own responses to literature would be to contradict and subvert the entire purpose of the study of literature. Form as such in literature is the arrangement of ideas in a particular order. To study form and ignore this significance reduces it to its mechanics and alienates the student, not to speak of the teacher, from his or her own vital interest, which to my mind is the study of ideas as a means of discovering order within them. When a student or teacher has the freedom to express, he or she is engaging in a study of ideas as order. It is a simple step from this response to the ideas and the forms they take in a particular text. I have found this to be so in practice.

All this flows from my own aesthetic theory and practice as poet, writer, and critic. . . . All good writing is teaching anyhow, but to teach apart from writing requires every bit as many tech-

nical and concrete approaches as does writing, and I have tried
to follow these principles faithfully from day to day.

We discussed poetry as the representation, by images and con-
crete situations, of states of mind and feeling. Association of im-
ages with one another, concrete situations with one another, or
images and situations in association with each other represents
thought or emotion in development—another way of saying that
narrative is at the root of the complete realization of an idea or
feeling, whether it takes the form of an association of images or
situations or combinations of both.

From this we went on to examine the basic nature of language
itself as picturization for ourselves of objects outside us or of
states of being within us. We pointed to cave writing and to Chi-
nese ideographs as words that still carry with them their original
denotations to a degree. However, all this was by way of proving
to ourselves that the making of poetry is in the very structure of
our method of thought: By association, that is, we seek for the
image or situation that will represent our states of mind.

Poetry, then, is a heightened version of our thought processes,
whether in our childhood or in our old age. Language, then, is the
means with which we seek to represent the images or situations.
As a consequence, language itself, from long use, needs constant
refurbishing and restructuring to be able to carry out its job effi-
ciently and vividly. For poets, the job is to watch their language
in conjunction with their thinking and to seek to give their think-
ing the integrity of language that truly represents it.

With these basic principles pinned down and agreed upon as a
whole among us, we proceeded to commune with our states of mind
or emotion and seek the exact representation in language. It came
as a refreshing relief to most of the participants, all of whom were
themselves teachers at high school, to find that they actually could
produce images and associations of images as new and charming
and connotative and uninhibited as the work of any child. The
minutes that were left before the close of the first session were

spent in reading our efforts aloud to each other. I concluded the session by repeating still another principle with which I had begun the session, one related directly to teaching—that the teacher should participate in any writing session he or she proposes in class and should offer his or her results to the class for its appreciation or criticism, along with the work of the students. Also, to encourage the students to write, the teacher should offer to tell a story orally, making one up on the spot, with all its blanks and successes; in other words, to identify with the story process itself and thus with the child's own natural state of mind thereby.

Oral storytelling, then, was to be encouraged among the students as a prelude to the actual writing. We held one such demonstration right in class, a teacher at the table at my encouragement improvising a story as I acted in the role of the listening child. Apparently, it was successful, as in conjunction with our discussion of the principles of poetry, the others found themselves writing their own fresh "representations" of the mood they were in at that moment. The class disbanded for the day with a high sense of achievement all around. Incidentally, I had written right along with the teachers in class, so that I found them very much at ease and un-self-conscious about their own efforts.

The second session dealt with two modes of poetry writing: the Objectivist and the Symbolist. I used my own work and that of Charles Reznikoff to show successful poems in both modes, and I urged the proposition that both modes were natural to children. The Objectivist mode, in which the person observes his or her environment and makes a judgment of it, would come with ease to a child because children are in a constant process of making judgments for their own learning and growth. The very process of judgment, then, implies a certain selection from among the materials of the environment on which the child would base his or her judgment or through which his or her judgment would be reflected. This was the Objectivist method in principle, and I read a group of Reznikoff's early Objectivist poems to illustrate how the method tends to select and arrange from experience to form or reflect usually a single judgment or insight into it.

I then turned to the teachers in the room and made them conscious of the very process going on in them at that moment—their judgments or insights into each other, into me, my judgment or insight into them—as the means we use with which to relate to each other by voice, manner, and action. It became apparent to them that this was actually what they were experiencing in their minds. I then recapitulated the thesis of the first session, that we are not so far removed from children's way of thinking as we in our adulthood imagine. In principle, our minds continue the same process of representing states of mind through external objects or events, but with increased awareness of choice, with increased sophistication of the process. We then set to writing in the Objectivist mode, writing from experience lived through in the past. Some of the teachers were more successful than others. All the work was read in class and commented on for its success in realizing the Objectivist mode. Several teachers promised to try the method with their students.

We then studied the Symbolist mode. I pointed out that there are symbols common to all of us and they are especially used by children, such as the tree, the rain, the moon, the sun. In urban areas, the colors black and white hold significance beyond their literal representation—the cop in the patrol car, for instance. While all these symbols are external to our thinking and could be used in the Objectivist mode, they also lend themselves to the Symbolist method, which seeks for another dimension, an internal one. We agreed that generally the Symbolist method tends to objectify internal states of mind, since symbols can be manipulated beyond their actual objective states as, for example, a moon could be made to dance or weep or the color black could be made to spread like a cloud over the entire sky. These arbitrary actions devised by the child or the poet reflect or present the self as the self is being grasped at that moment. In other words, we concluded, the differ-

ence between the Objectivist method and the Symbolist method
lies in the writer's orientation at the particular time. The Objectivist
method directs itself outward to external events while the Sym-
bolist method directs itself inward to internal states. The child,
like the adult, experiences both ways of perceiving and thinking,
but Symbolism in children's poetry is especially prominent if not
its main preoccupation. We attempted to write Symbolistically,
producing some fine examples. Once again the class session ended
with a strong sense of accomplishment.

The third and last session was a mixture of things. Several
teachers had brought in their students' work in the Symbolist
mode, which we looked at and found in several instances to be
tremendously exciting. I recapitulated the ideas discussed and
worked on during the last two sessions; the use of oral poetry or
oral improvisations by students and teachers in class; the need for
the teacher to participate with the students in writing poetry in
class; the teacher's identification with the students in the writing
of poetry; the use of the Objectivist and Symbolist methods; and
the principles of poetry that identify the teacher with the students.
I went on to introduce three additional modes of poetry writing.
I first described "found" poetry composed using newspapers or
magazines of any kind, that is, picking words and phrases at ran-
dom from articles and placing them into an arrangement that
conveys an entirely different meaning from what they originally
conveyed, with the purpose of creating kinds of poetry from these
arrangements. I illustrated with newspaper clippings and magazine
articles, taking words and phrases at random from articles on
science, business, education, and local and international events
and, inspired by the words and phrases themselves, combining
them into an arrangement such as appealed to me at the moment.
I then spoke of poetry written with a choice of words, preferably
verbs, nouns, adjectives, adverbs, and articles, made freely by the
student, who has to find the connectives with which the words
can be joined into a meaning of the student's own conceiving, with
the purpose of creating a whole poem. Lastly, I spoke of group

poetry, in which each member of the class, including the teacher, contributes a line of verse.

Each teacher then discovered found poetry in the newspapers and magazines we had brought with us in preparation for this method of writing. Apparently, it was one of the most enjoyable experiences in class, with several members participating with a zest that went beyond anything they had experienced in previous trials of writing. The class continued busily in this exercise, choosing words, headlines, phrases, and so forth, cutting them out of the pages and arranging them on sheets of typewriter paper, then pasting them carefully in place. I think it might prove to be the mode of writing that will be most popular among students, if I can judge from the enthusiasm of the teachers.

6. Poetry as a Vindication of the Self

The question I often ask myself, even today, which prompts me to talk about it, is whether there is a point to being a poet. I think about it and then sigh and ask myself what else is there for me to do? I've tried being in business. It was fun for a while, until I found myself, during periodic slowdowns, laying people off. It was then I knew I was not cut out for that sort of thing. I was not made to deal impersonally with people. As a businessman, I had the unfortunate weakness of making close friends with my employees, the very ones I would be giving the pink slips to. There were people in business to whom it meant absolutely nothing to fire others wholesale. I'd look at my face in the mirror in the washroom and see those tense lines from my nostrils to the down curve of my lips. I was already writing then, watching and telling myself of all that was happening to me and to others. Ten years of this kind of living, the direct opposite of what I felt life should be, and I managed to sell out lock, stock, and barrel. After paying off all debts and obligations, as I have noted, with no more than a week's salary in my pocket, I went in search of a position elsewhere as an employee. I was going to avoid the horrors of being an employer.

Did I succeed? As an employee in another owner's bindery, I had to look over my shoulder every time I took an action, such as stopping my machine to correct an error in the folding dimensions of a particular brochure that was being sent through the machine by the thousands for distribution in the mail. I would have to explain in detail to the supervisor, hovering in the vicinity with his pen and the work-time schedule used as a basis for pricing and/or evaluating the machine operator's efficiency. I was subject to constant surveillance. My situation, I began to understand, was exactly that of being an employer, in reverse. I was on the opposite end of the exchange. The difference between employer and employee was only a fine distinction. Each of us had to endure an impersonal and nonhuman relationship to the other and, by extension, to ourselves.

I was writing all the while and had just begun to read William Carlos Williams who, as I came to realize, had long ago recognized the situation for what it was, as he had said more than once about the average American life. The American life lived by most of us was plainly and wholeheartedly counter to the life of the emotions and the intellect or imagination. Just as he had written about it, challenged by its indifference to poetry, I found myself writing about it, similarly challenged by its resistance to everything but the simplest common denominator of routine thinking and doing. But writing about it while still on the job only served to make me even more unhappy with my situation, as my insights into the problems sharpened through writing about them.

Well, what was left? Teaching. Wendell Berry called me long distance from Lexington, Kentucky, in the early 1960s to ask me to take his place at the University of Kentucky that year, when he would be away on a Rockefeller fellowship. I took the offer.

The first few years were exciting. I loved teaching. I was endlessly drawn to it as the stimulant for my thinking about poetry, especially poems I had in mind to write. I'd think them through aloud in class, particularly classes in which I taught the writing of poetry or the study of a particular poet. I'd find myself engaged in a passionate debate with the work of the poet under study, analyzing every aspect of his or her poetry from my point of view as poet. Ideas that had been lying fallow or silent in the back of my mind during those trying years in business found themselves articulated right in class in my enthusiasm with my freedom to teach and to think aloud about what was closest to me. Ideas I hadn't even realized were in my thoughts—they had been so dimly perceived or felt for years—came forth in that moment of confrontation in class with the work of another poet. I'd go home and ponder these new revelations and start a poem that had these insights at its root. This went on for five exhilarating years and then, slowly, probably by the early seventies, I began to feel repetitious to myself and, shockingly to me, indifferent to the class.

It reminded me of my past life in the role of businessman, in that impersonal treadmill it had become for me; and now I was losing out as teacher, that which had rescued me from business, and as a result, losing out as poet too, since teaching had been such a strong inducement to writing. I also had to acknowledge, though, that after all, I had written a body of work during those exhilarating years that had become at least two books, with many more poems in reserve. Well, here I am nearing my third decade as a teacher, having managed to publish nine more volumes of poetry and several volumes of prose, with more to come, and I find my joy as a teacher renewed in the progress I see in my students. I've learned to become more interested in the student in class than in my own thinking on my problems as poet. I've learned how to turn that sense of repetitiousness and indifference in myself to the benefit of the student. In short, I've learned in class to become a teacher first and poet second. I've concentrated on the student and the student's world which, to my surprise and gratitude, gave me the impulse with which to continue to write, in that spirit of enquiry and patient understanding that I developed in class. In brief, teaching was able to deepen and broaden me.

Okay. It's now going on more than twenty-five years and teaching full-time had to stop. On retirement, I intended to devote as much time as I could to writing, to spending more time with myself, perhaps to catching up with themes and insights I may have had to postpone as a teacher. As you no doubt remember, however, I began this by asking myself the point of being a poet. Why, you may ask, would I be asking myself such a question after having had the good fortune to see most of my work published and commented on nationally and internationally? One, supposedly, should gather strength and self-confidence from such recognition and implied success. And so one does, and yet I can ask myself that question in a kind of sad, puzzled tone. Well, I suppose I am the only one who can answer for myself. It is a very personal problem, but not so far removed from the general concerns of most all of us. There's retirement from the relatively secure environment of teaching, from the ready-made audience of students with whom to share my thoughts and concerns about many things and issues other than poetry which, as an art, embraces so much more than the discussion of techniques or narrowly focused themes. There's the world outside the classroom, which concerns us all and is a world that, once you step into it, is filled with an overwhelming sense of chaos, especially for poets or artists, who work through form, imposed upon or found within their material. As poet, I find the world out of my control and in fact in control of me, as I feel it work upon me. In brief, the poet in the world feels no more significant than the average person, and it is a crushing blow to the poet's sense of importance to the world. No, not importance to you as individuals hearing a poet talk about his art and himself. Perhaps not to you, but individuals do not control events or opinions, and individuals are not happy with themselves either, for exactly those reasons I have cited for myself. Each of us, to one degree or another, feels overwhelmed, pushed to live without fuss or emotion. About our feelings of love and balance, rest and calm, beauty and moral order—all that a poet brings to the attention of the reader, all that a reader seeks in his or her life—we feel the pressure to bypass it all, to waive it in place of something that we find difficult to define but that exists in the air itself. It is a sense of indifference to the human condition, of the impersonal that we encounter in the very streets we walk through, those very same feelings I experienced in business and at one time in the classroom. And hanging over all of us is the threat of universal destruction which, perhaps, is one cause of our sense of despair with ourselves and one cause for the withdrawal that we feel from the personal, the emotional, the poetic in each of us.

As poet, this is the problem I raise for myself. And so what is the point of poetry? The point, first of all, I guess, is to stay alive in such an atmosphere as I have described. Otherwise, we cannot get to the bottom of our unhappiness. If anything can make us curious and wish to know, it is this special unhappiness, such as I feel now. I am curious to find out what it means to be a poet in these days requiring the sacrifice of one's identity to merely survive. We feel the change to that status coming on us and through us with, it seems, the speed of light. We think of what we once securely knew and loved, appreciated, and lived by as becoming a back number to living. That which we gathered to ourselves as our identity in things, persons, ideas, and feelings, feelings especially, we find losing credibility in our own eyes as the circumstances that made our identity possible are withdrawn from beneath our very feet, not by our doing but by others' and by more powerful circumstances than our private worlds.

Well, the poet who is there with you in all these slippery, gloomy conditions can ask himself, Hey, where am I going? What am I doing here? Am I going to find myself somewhere new? Apparently, I am alive, but how about living in some kind of peace and order? Am I arriving there? Will I arrive there? Is all this movement meant to get me there? And these questions are not necessarily thought by poets only. There are questions we all ask ourselves and because they are not unique to poets, it becomes the duty and the joy of poets, feeling at one with others, to make of these questions the point of writing their poems. Writing poetry has this impelling motivation. It is to take the world as it comes at you and give it an order of comprehension that is the poem itself. It is to make the world a poem of itself for each of us who still believes himself or herself to be an individual. Let me present one of my poems to this point:

The Sky Is Blue

Put things in their place,
my mother shouts. I am looking
out the window, my plastic soldier
at my feet. The sky is blue
and empty. In it floats
the roof across the street.
What place, I ask her.

The poem ends in a question, but it is its own answer, the fact that it presents the problem and gives it the coherence of one's concern. It is a poem of our deepest concerns made visible for contemplation by everyone. No, it is not worth living without that sense of having some influence over our lives, some way of manifesting our own judgment or will, even under the most terrifying of circumstances. In fact, it is inescapably the nature of humanity.

Let me offer an amusing example, if only to lighten the mood. Let us take, for example, the vaunted computer that ticks off our social security number, our health card number, our payroll number. We have numbers for every single thing in our lives. Look at the prices on items we buy. Look at our clothes size, hat size, shoe size. I ask, how come in civil life we are not yet called by a number instead of our name? It certainly would be logical in the course of things, as they are developing right before us. See how many Pauls, Teds, Franks, Joans, Marys, and Davids there are in the world. A number could accurately distinguish you from the next Mary or David down the street. Okay. Let's assume we have that system. Shall the poet write about it? Of course he will. How else could we bear with it, live beyond it to song, to poetry, to feeling that can't be numbered—that in the last analysis will never be numbered. Imagine someone in authority saying to you, "We want number so and so emotion from you performed by such and such a time." It can't be done. No authority in its right mind would even contemplate it. So feeling triumphs. At least for now, for the foreseeable future, poetry is the art of emotion.

But is it enough to live for emotion? No, we live to handle all the numbers of our life correctly. We take pleasure in carrying through every need that numbers force upon us and in turn we learn to manipulate them after we have become easily proficient at handling them accurately. We begin to see the opportunity of playing with them, of making them perform for us—what a turn-about—and we begin to breathe easily. We begin to enjoy manipulating these numbers: the price of this, the price of that, the interest from this, the interest from that. It becomes a life in itself, and we find that it gives us a consciousness of ourselves in control, which is to say we can begin to define ourselves in relation to something that is not ourselves, by which we see clearly who we are, who we can further be.

But along comes a landslide of new numbers, and we seem once more overwhelmed, buried beneath them. Our breathing becomes difficult. What to do? Well, if it isn't death coming for us, say the number of ninety-years-of-age or one bullet or six-divorces-in-a-row or a deduction-from-our-salary-to-zero or an increase in the cost of rent-food-clothing-medicine, which bankrupts us and sends us out into the street with our furniture; if it isn't any of these numbers—and even if it is—do you lose your sense of outrage, sadness, or irony that you, with the collaboration of the millions of others like yourself, supported and contributed to a way of life, only to make life nearly impossible for all of us? It brings emotion back in full force. It becomes time to see and think and write of that which is essentially ourselves, at the very center of our being; that which could destroy us, for we can as easily become our own self-destructive engine as our own benefactor. And will poets write and sing and perform this truth? They will, until we are no more. They will because feeling is everpresent. It defines our humanness to ourselves, for we wish always to be defined as human, even under the worst conditions.

I offer no happy solutions to our nature. I offer simply the possibility of the poet to speak for all of us. The point of poetry, if shaky and trembling before the god-awful facts—the anti-poetic, if you wish to say so—is here with us to stay until it departs with the last man and woman from the face of the earth.

II. The Many in the One

7. My Life
with Whitman

One wonders what further there is to say about Whitman's poems after the publication of Justin Kaplan's *Walt Whitman: A Life* and Paul Zweig's *Walt Whitman: The Making of a Poet,* both of which deal with his work and with Whitman encyclopedically and in depth. One should not forget the earlier authoritative volume by Gay Wilson Allen, which, it can be said, formed the foundation for almost everything that has since been uncovered about Whitman and his poems. Such an array of information and insight leaves someone like me only one avenue for exploration and that is the subjective. No doubt, Whitman would have approved. That exploration is of the history of my encounter with his writings. It is an account that could be called my life with Whitman, embracing an everchanging perspective on him and on myself and my own writing in relation to him and his writings, changes that take place with life experience, with the practice of writing, and with getting to know the world and oneself in a dialogue with society and its culture. And yet each of us who is steeped in Whitman's work and ideas knows how much he encompasses. One wonders even in a literary autobiography, such as this, whether that, too, has not already been lodged somewhere in his poems or between the lines, leaving one, to paraphrase the last line of "I Sit and Look Out," to 'see, hear and [be] silent.'

Still, as have so many, I am willing to take the chance to speak of the history of my relationship in the belief that it will contribute to the universal affirmation of the poems' timelessness and their enduring influence.

At about fifteen, I realized with amazement that a man like Whitman had lived, a man who had lifted himself from the drudgery of routine to exult in himself, in his senses, in his society, and in the faces, bodies, minds, and thoughts of its people, when I, then fifty years after his death, was, yes, as obsessively occupied with self, but with a difference. The difference was anger. I had vowed to make my way as a poet despite my family's objections and resistance and other obstacles placed before me, obstacles such as duty, necessity, compassion, and love. Still, was I not the same essentially in spirit as Whitman, as he was so tireless in pointing out in his poems? Did I not share the same aspiration for myself and for society and its people that I had come to learn and accept and identify with in reading his poems? Unfortunately, what I learned about myself from his poems and what I learned, sadly, from my circumstances made, to say the least, an ironic juxtaposition and bitter comment in confrontation with what I was beginning to experience in the real world. I am speaking of the start of the Great Depression, 1929, the year of my discovery of Whitman.

My first experience of Whitman's poems took place in a junior high school class, with the teacher intoning "Crossing Brooklyn Ferry" as my classmates and I followed the text in our anthology. Here was language that escaped the confines of our daily bread-and-butter existence, language that flew above my head, that wanted to carry me with it. I was breathless hearing it read aloud. I was with Whitman on the ferry, I was with him in his foreboding of death and in his projection of his sense of immortality onto others, particularly onto me at that moment. I was he viewing the crowds aboard the ferry and ships in the harbor. I was mouthing his words to the future, which was now in me, that told me he was here in this classroom, speaking, his presence an awesome light in my head. It was light with a force that could, if I let it, lift me from my seat. I sat quietly, not wanting to be taken by classmates as strange, as overly excited, or as behaving like a child, though I wasn't much more than a child. My training, my upbringing had instructed me to remain perfectly silent and still, to be observant but disciplined, alert but obedient. Whitman's poems had some-how blocked that conditioning and so I had to keep a tight hold on my seat, while inside I was as though empty but free.

How I came upon his poems again later is a story in itself. It began with an interest in Carl Sandburg and William Carlos Williams, both of whom I had read in Louis Untermeyer's anthology, the very same one from which my teacher had intoned "Crossing Brooklyn Ferry." As I was to read in the anthology, these two poets had been influenced by Whitman. Nevertheless, I read both poets with a certain detached interest. Their language came close to mine; Williams, especially, caught me, and I read on. That these two poets had been brought to realization as poets by the poems of Whitman led me to consider that perhaps I could return to Whitman with the same kind of detached interest with which I read Williams and Sandburg. And I read them as I might read the newspaper, with the same ease, though neither wrote in an idiom akin to journalese. The two poets wrote in the everyday spoken word, Williams much more emphatically. It made their writing a "quick read." Besides, that they wrote in contemporary speech en-couraged me to think it possible to bring my own spoken word, in short, my sensibility, to a reading of Whitman's poems, in the ex-pectation of shielding myself from being once again overwhelmed as I had been in that junior high class. My way of looking at and thinking about things and people in the language I was condi-tioned to would become the means with which I could screen out Whitman's language, tone and rhythm yet absorb something of his spirit and ideas without losing my identity in his. I checked out his *Complete Poems* from the local library and read and held on to my seat firmly, bearing in mind the writings of Williams and Sandburg. I could still feel my head wanting to rise, and so I knew that I had yet to learn how to restrain this urge to be carried away by his poems, while still living with them. I knew too that I had to remain my own person, as had Williams and Sandburg in rela-tion to him.

Nevertheless, in my voyage through the poems of Whitman I

began to dispose of Sandburg as ballast. I began to see that he read like a poor imitation. For me, there was no lift to Sandburg's words. Rather, his was a kind of hortatory shouting. Nor did he have that fierce tenderness of language that was Whitman's, or that open-eyed wonder at the world and its people. He was stark. His poems seemed often protest poems, with an occasional side glance at moments to celebrate or to enjoy. Nonetheless, I had felt myself drawn to his poems because they reflected something of my own circumstance, the unhappiness with the treadmill ordinariness of daily routine and its attendant hardships. At fifteen I had just begun to work weekends as stock clerk for the Wanamaker store. Still, for me, Sandburg spoke too loudly and too insistently, rattling the language rather than exciting it. I could still remember myself in childhood coming upon a toy I had been neglecting only to pick it up and drop it again, realizing its limitations for me. Sandburg's poems were something to come upon incidentally. I dropped him, giving him my distant affection.

Williams's poems were another matter. Though I could read him with the same detachment with which I had read Sandburg, there was a difference. Williams spoke to me directly, at the level of conversation, in a voice I could associate with my own, making me his contemporary and confidant. I was curious but I was reserved. Just as I had wanted to remain detached from Sandburg, so I did not want to share myself with Williams either. Williams's language, so much like mine—matter of fact and to the point— carried with it the unhappiness with which I was confronting my circumstances. If his poems were poetry, I told myself, I was in a dilemma. In my initial exploration of writing, I did not believe the right mode could be the idiom in which I spoke. My thoughts and desires were with Whitman and his language. In his language I felt freedom.

Nevertheless, before I could launch myself upon Whitman's style without becoming absorbed into it, I first had to understand how and why it worked, so that I could develop a certain detachment from it, yet at the same time gain through the style my own inspiration. I had to find the key to his method so I could preserve my equilibrium. I began to read him as a discipline, and it seemed to me, holding him mentally at a distance, that he was addressing a being, someone perhaps in himself, perhaps someone apart from him (could it be me and others?) who knew everything, who loved and gave love to everything. That couldn't quite be me, nor could it be those I knew in school or at home or at my weekend job. Could he be addressing himself, making love to himself? That was how I remembered my childhood, when I would catch myself at times in the open air under a keen blue sky at play with friends or simply breathing in the air of spring, inspiring me with myself, in love with my exaltation and expansive mood toward others who I felt had to resemble me in my exaltation. I was filled with the satisfaction of being who I was. It had to be so for my friends, also, I believed, or I would be too much alone in it. It was a happiness that needed to be shared for me to enjoy and love it as I did.

But how true was this for me in the life I was leading, challenging myself to answer for having been swayed by exciting words? Were they a drug I was taking to deceive myself, to calm me in my rightful angers and fears? The time was the early thirties, and I was now eighteen, in the grip of industry and doing heavy physical labor full time at my father's bindery in Lower Manhattan for the sake of food and shelter. For these I had to endure the monotony of repetitive, exhausting manual labor. Instead of making life the dream it was in Whitman's poems, I had to ask myself whether life was worth the effort at all in view of these hardships.

I set Whitman aside again. Reading him in the midst of my travail was too much like baiting myself. It increased my anger, for which I had no outlet. I still had to eat and have shelter, and so I still had to do heavy labor, the only kind available to me then. I was caught in some kind of trap not of my own making but of my resolve to survive. I could find no solution in Whitman to persuade me to feel differently about myself, to feel instead as he did about himself and as I had felt in childhood before I was introduced to manual labor. Then, in my naivete, I believed I should have been devoting myself to joyful recreation with companions or, as Whitman would have it, loafing and inviting my soul. His panegyric on labor, as he wrote of it in the ideal sense of his thought, collapsed for me in the reality of a twelve-hour working day six days a week.

Though I set his poems aside, I continued to write. It was not with the afflatus of excited speech. It was closer to the bitter portraits of myself and of others in Whitman's beloved Manahatta, the site of frenzied, driven commercialism. With little that I could do to keep myself from being engulfed in commercial life, I became hostile to Whitman's poetry and expressed as much in poems satirizing his exaltations, parodying his language to tragic reversal of its theme of the triumph of self-realization. It was that period in the thirties when well-dressed men and women were standing in line for hours waiting to be fed from street soup kitchens. Had I been fired from my job, I would have found myself in that very same line. With such conditions surrounding me on every side, I knew Whitman was of no help to me. When I did occasionally sneak a look at his poems because of my residual love for them, it was because of a longing for my childhood and illusions of my early youth. Disappointed, I would put down his book again. His poems did not seem relevant. They did not help to rescue me from my difficult life as, in all innocence, I believed they should have.

But was I right in wanting him to rescue me, I would ask myself in moments of clarity. Evidently not, since, looking realistically at my problems, I saw he could not help in any practical way. The fault had to be mine, I had to acknowledge, in expecting such help. Whitman's poems were a vision, as I was forced to recognize, and as such, could not be applied to fact.

In 1933, I had been trying my hand at writing short stories. One story that was published that year, for which in 1934 I received a citation, led to that reporter's job on the WPA newspaper. I found myself beginning to relax from my desperate mood. I could turn back to Whitman's poems, as if to tally my experience against the poems and to come up with an overall meaning and purpose for

his writing that would be broader and deeper than simply a prac-
tical help, a guide book to success in the work-a-day world.

Not until twenty years later, in 1954, did I have the first sus-
tained opportunity to think through to such a meaning. I took on
the editorship of a special issue of the *Beloit Poetry Journal* in
celebration of the one hundredth year, 1955, of the publication of
the *Leaves of Grass*. I was to collect poems from American poets
who, like me, related to Whitman's work. In conjunction with the
efforts of these poets, I would seek for my own understanding of
this visionary giant. I would seek an accommodation, a reciprocity
as one adult to another. Whitman, too, in his time had experienced
the worst—a divided, bleeding nation—and he had lived through it
to write the poem of the nation's survival, "When Lilacs Last in
the Dooryard Bloomed," on the assassination of his beloved presi-
dent, as well as later poems and prose on his still fervent hope for
a new world. For me to undertake the editorship of that special
issue meant once again to submit myself as student before teacher,
to insights, lessons, and affirmations learned from him.

Ironically, I had been chosen for this editorial role despite the
satires I had written of his work, because of the profound influence
he had exerted on me. It was clear to the editors that I had not
given up my identification with working people but that I was ex-
pressing contention between two opposing ways of living and per-
ceiving. Both ways were within me: first, the way of the grinding
routine of the ordinary in which for years I had earned my living.
It placed me physically and in spirit in proximity to the average
man. Second, that way of the poet who somehow had to accom-
modate to such a life. I had to accommodate myself especially if,
as poet, I was to enjoy a Whitman-like embrace of others. Here
was a paradox I could not resolve. By their very nature—that of
the poet, contemplative and reclusive in order to write, and that of
the poet as workingman on the assembly line—the ways contra-
dicted and opposed one another. Trapped in the daily grind, the
poet could not realize himself without losing Whitman's vision.
His poetic sensibility had to rise beyond the daily concerns of bread

and butter to see life in its eternal manifestations, though, paradoxically, it had to do so in appreciation and celebration of that ordinary life. This was Whitman's transcendent vision. It was a truth to which I had to humble myself. I was a rebellious son, but I, too, aspired to self-realization within his concept.

My fellow poets who contributed to the *Beloit Poetry Journal* special issue were, like me, in Whitman's camp and were, like him, being neglected by the academics, who had excluded them from anthologies for class study. The fifties were a far cry from the twenties, when Untermeyer had published Whitman, Williams, and Sandburg. All three poets had been virtually eliminated from courses in American poetry in most of our prestigious schools. Whitman, when taught, was taught as an object lesson in exaggerated, inflated, imprecise style. I invited such poets as Louis Zukofsky, Edwin Honig, Charles Olson, Langston Hughes, William Carlos Williams himself, and others to contribute. On receiving my invitation, they did so mostly with enthusiasm. Yet they were skeptical and even sad that Whitman, on the hundredth anniversary of the *Leaves of Grass,* would receive little or no attention beyond this special issue, except for the collection of essays titled *Leaves of Grass, One Hundred Years Later,* edited by Milton Hindus, with contributions from Williams, Richard Chase, Kenneth Burke, David Daiches, Leslie Fiedler, J. Middleton Murry, and Hindus himself.

It was in such a situation, with Whitman relatively isolated among respected critics and scholars, that I was beginning a whole new relationship with his poems and with myself. For me, it was to be the one in the many, the many in the one, after all. That was what I would have to struggle with from then on. That had been the message to me in my early youth, to find myself like others and to feel liberated from my isolated self in that finding—that is, to feel empowered by this mass of so many like myself. Of course, it was but one aspect of Whitman's vision but the one that led me to yet greater resolution.

Thus I learned to respect, admire, and believe, if reluctantly, in what Whitman had to say, what his poems were urging upon me. Oddly enough, I had already for some years been apprenticing myself to Williams, having gone through my initial distaste for his poems, which in language and observation had brought me smack up against my own sordid urban experience in that heavenly city of Whitman's, Manahatta. With the language of *Leaves of Grass* not useful to my twenieth-century sensibilities, with Sandburg too loud and obvious, with Hart Crane's exaltations irrelevant to my own reality, I was left with no choice but to turn to Williams for companionship and self-affirmation, much as I disliked his poems. They kept me locked into my own life without, I felt, offering me an out in either style or thought. To follow his style meant to accept the situation I was in and to make poetry of it, but to me at that time poetry meant art as a means with which to reject city life, to remove myself from it in language that had nothing in common with the city's savage idiom. Williams, on the other hand, had decided to confront the situation directly, to let his poems reflect the idiom in wonder and appreciation of what was, for him, its strange beauty. I argued with myself: Did not Williams somewhere write of his first attachment and love of poetry in the poems of Keats, who in his poems fled the world? I had read that Williams was a doctor practicing his skills among patients in the very depths of the slums, patients riddled with unhappiness and disease, with poverty and anger, drink and dissoluteness. In further pursuit of his thinking, I learned that he had written of these conditions in stories also. He, too, knew the worst, as had Whitman, and as I did, and yet he persisted in working among and writing of these forlorn people in their humanity. His poems startled me with their celebration of the uniqueness of shanty houses; broken sidewalks; broken, strewn glass; pathetic flower pots on the windowsills of slum tenements. Williams was affirming life in the mass. He was not afraid, or repelled, or unhappy, only angry that such had to be the lives of people who for all their suffering and degradation, were no different, no less human than himself.

Here was a modern Whitman, but in the language of our times.

It was language unsparing in its portrayal of harshness, yet it had
its exaltation and excitement. It induced the reader to live with the
people and with Williams in his experiencing. This was akin to
Whitman of the Civil War poems and of the earlier poems: "Song
of Myself" and "The Sleepers." Here was a resolution of the diffi-
culty I had made for myself. To live and write had to be one and
the same process, as it had been for Whitman, as it was for Wil-
liams. Only then would the poet be liberated from division and
despair. As poet I could master my own being through acting in
good faith toward my subject, my circumstances, though bound by
these same circumstances. Beyond stood the greater truth of the
existence we lived in common as it revealed itself in the individ-
ual. As poet I could take comfort in and draw strength from know-
ing it was mine to recognize and to believe:

> The impalpable sustenance of me from all things, at
>   all hours of the day,
> The simple, compact, well-joined scheme—myself
>   disintegrated, every one disintegrated, yet part
>   of the scheme,
> The similitudes of the past, and those of the future,
> The glories strung like beads on my smallest sights
>   and hearings—on the walk in the street, and
>   the passage over the river,
>
> (Crossing Brooklyn Ferry, 1860)

The aspiration toward such self-realization had to take place
through the trials, sufferings, and engagements with one's time
and place and people. I could now read Whitman through the
poems of Williams, for in many of Williams's poems I could read
his struggle to write in order to define himself against and beyond
his confining circumstance, as for example, in the poem "Danse
Russe":

> If when my wife is sleeping
> and the baby and Kathleen
> are sleeping
> and the sun is a flame-white disc
> in the silken mists
> above shining trees,—

if I in my north room
dance naked, grotesquely
before my mirror
waving my shirt round my head
and singing softly to myself:
"I am lonely, lonely,
I was born to be lonely,
I am best so!" If I admire my arms, my face,
my shoulders, flanks, buttocks
against the yellow drawn shades,—

Who shall say I am not
the happy genius of my household?"

And so that which had moved me in my childhood and youth in "Crossing Brooklyn Ferry" had now returned in my maturity in a manner I could deal with. I now had a clear understanding and acceptance of what had impelled me toward Whitman's poems again and again through the years, as often as I rejected them, however sadly.

As an American poet having spent a long and difficult apprenticeship to Whitman, I may say that his vision is in the very weave of American thought and life. I take myself as one proof of it. We need only turn to other American poets of the twentieth century, Muriel Rukeyser, Allen Ginsberg, Diane Wakoski, Galway Kinnell, James Wright, Robert Bly, Gary Snyder, to name but a few whose work is unquestionably based on Whtiman's achievement.

Whitman is our heritage. I see my poems as part of an effort to affirm his gift through the independence of my style, an independence he encouraged by his celebration of the individual, within the fragmentation of society and culture we are undergoing today. It was division as it expressed itself in his time which Whitman addressed. As he was to acknowledge indirectly in "Democratic Vistas" and elsewhere, his vision bore no fruit in society, in politics, or even in literature in his time and for years thereafter. Yet his poems are at the root of our concept of an ideal American society. That we continue in that vision in our own works constitutes the evidence we have not yet given up on his message.

Still, as is the case with many other poets, I feel impelled to
state in my own work that we are not yet bound outward toward
wholeness with one another or with ourselves. Precisely the oppo-
site is true, if I may take myself as a representative example. It
takes a constant struggle to strive for wholeness in significant ways
in a culture and a society almost single-mindedly concentrated on
the single, separate person, surely an ironic echo of one of Whit-
man's famous phrases. We are asked to be on our own, each of us,
and to celebrate this individuality, cut off from one another, often
with disastrous consequences. Still, that famous phrase was meant
as but one leg of the entire structure. The individual, as I have
learned the hard way, is part of the whole, with an inborn "adhe-
siveness" toward others. We belong to one another if only because
we manifest the same energy of existence. We are, finally, the same
being:

> I celebrate myself
> and what I assume you shall assume
> for every atom belonging to me as good belongs to you.
> (Song of Myself, 1855)

While for me it is the ultimate truth, I know that like so many
others, I am constantly failing to appreciate and act on that truth.
I turn inward instead, toward my so-called private self, under the
pressure of society and its skewed culture, and also, it must be said,
under the pressure of that certain sense of singleness with which
we are born. Still, to give in and remain enclosed and indifferent
to others, and, finally, to become indifferent to ourselves as a result,
spells death. And so I hold before me as guidestar those opening
lines of "Song of Myself." In striving to achieve such a wholeness
of realization in my relationships with others and with myself,
though I note more failure than success, I gain my dignity and
self-respect from the striving itself. Though I will never achieve
an ideal state nor, for that matter, do I expect it to happen in our
divided culture and society, the key is in the effort, to paraphrase
Whitman in his later years. In the determination to transcend, one
is free of the pressure of failure.

And so, Whitman still is motivating me. If what I seek of life is ultimately unattainable, in the written word I keep alive the hope. I find release from my limitations, momentarily at least, in my poems addressed to that hope in every form, tone, spirit, and subject, and so it is for American poets today and for those to come.

I see my relationship to Walt Whitman as that of a dissident son to an overdemanding father. He demands, as he does of himself, total allegiance to a transcendental version of existence. I can't see it, especially not on or in his terms. Quite possibly, if he had lived long enough to see the technological advances in space exploration, he would have begun to sense our isolation in the universe, which would have given him an altogether different and desolating view of humankind's relationship to the universe and to itself, the view with which most of us hold; and so while I look on him as a totally affectionate father, one from whom I learned how to free myself from the constraint of given ideas and behavior patterns, not only in poetry but in life too, I cannot accept his acceptance of nineteenth-century piety in relation to a godhead, nor to a vision of so-called progress, nor a vision of the perfection of man, nor of man's ultimate union in brotherhood. He has lost me there, and yet I deeply regret the loss and sometimes find myself expecting the miracle to happen. Whitman is great because he has given us these issues to debate, to resolve, central to our own existence. His genius as poet all of us now take for granted, even certain academicians but, of course, with their kind of distortion peculiar to ideologues, which is their main virtue. It's not a poetic virtue so that by applying their theories to Whitman's work we no longer recognize Whitman as a poet, but this is another story in my "quarrel" with Whitman, who now has been taken over by the academicians.

⚜ 8. Finding Wallace Stevens ⚜

I can recall the first discussion of Wallace Stevens's work I had with a friend, the poet Armand Schwerner. We were driving home together in his car from a short celebration, a spring festival in a park situated downtown on the New York harbor. How we got into the discussion I can't recall, but I do remember that Armand at that time, the early sixties, was deeply wrapped up in Stevens's poems, and I had just come across them again for the third or fourth time, with about the same sense of distance and aversion—yes, aversion.

Armand kept comparing Stevens to Whitman. It was so far from my thinking on Stevens that I nearly became ill with anger at this misrepresentation of Whitman, this association with a poet who, to my reading, had absolutely no interest in the life around him, who cared little for people, who spoke of life and its events in the abstract generally or attempted baroque jokes about it. At the time, Whitman completely occupied my thoughts. I saw no way to write a poetry of this nation without reference to Whitman and his manner—at least to speak openly and concretely of the life we were living, in the voice I was given. I had learned that much from Whitman. To me, this is what was meant by "his manner."

I had gained the freedom to write as I was writing from the example set by Whitman, as derived from the vernacular and subjects of his time. Armand continued in his calm voice to try to show me how Stevens, in his way too, had gained freedom of style and subject—following Whitman philosophically. That, to me, was impossible to prove, and we dropped the discussion after about an hour. I had grown heated emotionally. Armand was driving, and had to remain calm, with his eyes fixed on the road, but it was clear to me, as it was to him, not only that we disagreed but that I had, apparently, revealed something to myself of which I had not been aware until then. I was fearful of the ideas and manner of such a poet as Stevens. They seemed to threaten me directly. They were not the subjects and speech with which I was most comfortable. Stevens, in his position in life, had the freedom to write of entirely different subjects and in a manner that, in my opinion, virtually removed him from the mainstream of American poetry. Furthermore, here was Armand, with my same life-style and background, allowing himself to become absorbed in the aristocratic, elite Symbolist writing Stevens practiced. I asked my-self silently whether I too was not vulnerable to Stevens's influ-ence if Armand already had succumbed. It was as if an enemy of mine had learned how to undermine the very allies on whom I had to depend to feel authentic and strong in my own life.

Obviously, I was not yet up to the complexity of thought that had gone into Stevens's poems, and I was confusing his style of embellishment with some sort of unconscious connection with the luxury of his upper-middle-class existence. The discussion left me dissatisfied with myself. Respecting Armand, despite my strong difference with him, I felt I had to look further into this issue between us. I let the whole matter simmer in the back of my mind. I knew that I had to examine my whole life first to reaffirm, if possible, the values I had gained from Whitman. I had to measure them against what I had almost against my will learned to under-stand about Stevens from Armand's calm disputation with me. I had to acknowledge to myself reluctantly that Stevens was saying in so many words, all of his own colorful choosing, that this world we are living in could not satisfy a man's whole appetite for liv-ing, and that too was my own implied grief, as it ran through my poems beneath an open, self-affirming tone, that yet lent a sadness to them. It was very much because of the life I was living that my poems, which had begun in celebration, had to turn back in sadness. If Stevens had to express the same thought in more exuberant style, it was because he felt personally that he had to defy the grayness that his eyes met everywhere. When I realized this, I took up Stevens's work again and began to read it from a new perspective, accepting his Symbolist technique, his allusive disjunctions and abstractions and his often involuted, arbitrary syntax. I understood and was grateful I had found him out at last.

9. Finding William Carlos Williams

After my first meeting with William Carlos Williams, I realized, but only later, its emblematic importance to me. At that first meeting, in 1949, at the YW-YMHA on 92nd Street, he read from my poems, praising their structure and style to an audience of poets who were silent and attentive. The occasion had been advertised as being Williams's reading from his own poems, but he chose to begin by reading from mine. I could not absorb the significance of this for me as a poet just starting out; I was more stunned than aware. Eventually I understood its contribution to my sense of self as a poet, after I began to submit poems to magazines and to find many rejected out of hand, along with an occasional negative lecture from the editor, usually on poems I considered among my best. Depressed, I would find myself thinking back to Williams's public praise. He also reviewed my first book, *Poems,* for the *New York Times Sunday Book Review.* I took his praise as my cornerstone, and gradually recovered. I went on to mail these same poems rejected to other magazines.

What followed was, to say the lease, ironic. It became a bitter experience for us both. One day I received a letter from Williams that was filled with anger and despair. *Partisan Review* had rejected a section from *Paterson.* He asked me to find a publisher for the piece, then a three-page preface to Book 3 of *Paterson.** He was at a loss to think of any magazine that would accept it. His sense of himself as a successful poet was at a low ebb. I was

* It was published in *12th Street: A Quarterly* 23, No. 1 (December 1949), pp. 9–11.

staggered. I had been writing in his protective shade, so to speak, building upon his techniques. He was my mentor. Yet he had received a deeply damaging blow, and it implicated my status also. It was from his support and praise of my work that, in large part, I had gained my confidence as a poet. I recovered angrily, determined to do something to help, to help myself as it seemed, in the process. Luckily, I was then associated indirectly with the magazine *12th Street: A Quarterly,* published by the New School for Social Research, edited by Morris Weisenthal, friend and poet. Weisenthal was enthusiastic about receiving Williams's work. Williams mailed a copy of the rejected passage to me, and it was subsequently published. I became alert to the vociferous debate underway among competing aesthetes, particularly as it applied to *The Partisan Review,* and I could see that the shield of support that Williams had given me was now broken, and that he was angry and embattled himself.

Around 1961, I received news of his second stroke, from which by the time I heard of it he was making a shaky recovery. Denise Levertov and I arranged to take the bus to his home at Rutherford. It was not to be a pleasant visit for me. It was difficult for him to speak and when he did it was with a certain bitterness and querulousness I had never before associated with him. In my meetings and correspondence with him he had usually been open, energetic, forthright, and positive. I was upset by his changed condition. I thought back to his letter of despair because of *The Partisan Review* rejection.

He was very fond of Denise and asked her to read a poem of hers he liked immensely. It was an excellent poem, referring to or originating in a dream. I can't remember exactly which poem it was. I remember now that it dealt with a love experience in very sensuous terms. Williams listened, nodded enthusiastically, then turned to ask me sharply why I couldn't write a poem as physically stirring as hers. Denise, seated at his feet, was shocked at his attack and quickly came to my defense. But he turned to me again and repeated the question. By this time I had recovered, gratified by

Denise's defense, and replied coolly that I didn't have to write that way because I lived that way, or words to that effect. He grinned and looked at me more closely. Denise urged him to listen to a poem of mine. He agreed and I read the poem "Guilt" from *Say Pardon.* He found it thoughtful. It was as if I had been able to put myself in his favor again. I was vastly relieved but with a residue of bitterness, as if somehow I had been betrayed in my trust of the man. But I overlooked it because I could see, as we all could, that he was not himself. One half of his mouth was crooked from the stroke. He had to be helped to and from his chair. He was keen enough to sense his own physical deterioration. He had great difficulty in enunciating his words and Flossie, his wife, tried not to let him speak too much or with the vehemence that came into his voice. Denise and I left shortly after, both very sad. I knew I had seen him for the last time. He was really too weak for company, and the prognosis for the future was bleak.

Williams and I had come to the end of our road together. He could no longer be the emblematic support I still craved, and I was no longer someone he could praise unconditionally. We were parting as two poets struggling, he for his life and breath, and I at a loss in my grief for him and for myself, set apart from him forever to lead my own committed life as it would unfold out of the shadow of Williams.

~ 10. William Carlos Williams ~ and Wallace Stevens: Two of a Kind

The path I follow here comes of my increasing knowledge and understanding of the aesthetic relationship between two great American poets, William Carlos Williams and Wallace Stevens, a relationship I ultimately came to recognize as organic to and, I believe, symbiotic with the fiber, strength, and future of American poetry. To explain how I arrived at this conclusion requires an autobiographical account, beginning with my earliest reading of both poets in my youth. It was a gradual unfolding, with its sudden leap of discovery, as will happen at times to scientists who putter around for years with their instruments and theories until suddenly one day or night the revelation that has been implicit all the while dawns upon them. And last I must confess I write best in the autobiographical mode when I am dealing with ideas and perceptions, for they become true for me only as they are concretely manifested in my own life.

In my reading and study of the lives and works of these two poets and of some of the correspondence between them, my one insight or revelation came in a leap of discovery.

Whether this leap is an illusion or peculiar to me, I leave to others to judge. It is a subjective truth, which I must respect in myself because of the urgency in me to believe in it and to communicate it as I would do after having written a poem. Perhaps what I have written here is a passionate prose poem. It shaped itself naturally around a metaphorical allusion.

My life with Stevens: it began with repugnance. At that time I was deep in my life with Williams. But, oddly, my life with Williams also began with repugnance, strangely enough, for his language, which was so distinctly the opposite in tone and style from that of Stevens. I had come upon Williams's poems at least several years before coming upon the poems of Stevens. I was in my teens. Like Williams in his earliest period, in my youth I was writing in the manner of the revolutionary romantic poets of the first half of the nineteenth century, Shelley in particular. It was years since Williams had gone through his apprenticeship to Keats; he already was writing with a savagery and a downright "ugliness" of language, as I then perceived it, that I could not distinguish from the daily talk everywhere around me, as for example, in the following poem in part, "The Trees," an early experimental work in sound and measure:

> The trees—being trees
> thrash and scream
> guffaw and curse—
> wholly abandoned
> damning the race of men—
>
> Christ, the bastards
> haven't even sense enough
> to stay out of the rain—
>
> Wha ha ha ha
>
> Wheeeee
> Clacka tacka tacka
> tacka tacka
> Wha ha ha ha ha
> ha ha ha

What? This was poetry, I asked myself in dismay, modern, advanced poetry? I had had enough. But I was just beginning my life in the factories and offices of Manhattan, and so my life with Shelley was becoming smeared with the very same sludge that Williams had shaped so vigorously into a poem. Shelley simply did not belong in this dreadful place. I could feel the absurdity when I wrote in his idealized, seraphic language. Shelley simply did not comport in manner or idea with the raw, as I then thought, sewage to which I was being exposed. And I realized, partly in horror and partly in determination, that for me to live and to survive in this environment I had to discover the langauge that corresponded to what I was undergoing. Finding it would at least be a beginning toward a truth with which I could then live, ugly as it was going to be; and so once more, this time girding myself, I turned to Williams and saw, at last, what he was about. Well, by that time, Yeats too had become important to me for his specific, hard-edged colloquial writing, and so the transition to Williams was made that much easier for me. I could see that what Williams was doing was in its way Yeatsian, taking the rag-and-bone shop of the city and giving it the luster, the glow, and the power trans-figured by his poetic being. It was the beginning of my life with Williams. Although I was still heady with the perfume of Shelley's poems, I was ready for an honest breath of fresh air.

But there was Stevens to contend with. Some time had elapsed since I had separated myself from the romantics, and I was com-fortably and exuberantly domiciled with the poems and essays of Williams, almost totally immured by his work from my Shelleyan delusions, such as the language that flew above the heads and lives of those of whom I tried to speak, myself included. With Wil-liams, I was at ground zero, walking through the melee of revolt-ing sights, sounds, and situations, yet needing to hold it all in mind so as to produce it to my satisfaction as a poem, my ex-perience at last finding its expression in face-to-face confrontation with itself in language that reflected that experience, yet tran-scended it with a meaning of my own. While I was writing, it could release me into a world of my own, the liberating truth of it.

But again there was Stevens, who puzzled and angered me as I came upon his poems and essays, for example, "The Emperor of Ice Cream":

> Call the roller of big cigars,
> The muscular one, and bid him whip

In kitchen cups concupiscent curds.
Let the wenches dawdle in such dress
As they are used to wear, and let the boys
Bring flowers in last month's newspapers.
Let be be finale of seem.
The only emperor is the emperor of ice cream.

Take from the dresser of deal,
Lacking the three glass knobs, that sheet
On which she embroidered fantails once
And spread it so as to cover her face.
If her horny feet protrude, they come
To show how cold she is, and dumb.
Let the lamp affix its beam.
The only emperor is the emperor of ice cream.

Into this poem I read Stevens's contempt for the ordinary life
faced with the gravity of death. The language, for all its brilliance,
offended me. I gathered that Stevens, in his emphasis on a kind
of play with language in the manner of the grand seigneur, was
little concerned with the actual lives of people, of men like myself
who labored to secure for the family and self the good things in
life. In the period of the Great Depression, when I was in my early
twenties, what did we most mean by the good things in life? Sim-
ply this—food and shelter; ours was a preoccupation bordering on
fear; it lasted, for my generation into the forties. I had to ask
myself how Stevens had escaped the perplexities of unemployment
and short rations. It was a mystery to me. Yet that he, too, was
aware of the social calamity that had come upon us I was in no
doubt. Others of his poems obliquely acknowledged the fact. That
obliqueness was the problem. It carried with it an air of separate-
ness and an otherworldliness with no relation to persons like my-
self and the many with whom I had aligned myself.

Stevens, I had to conclude, was just a playboy among words,
words that according to my relationship with Williams should
have passionately and honestly transcribed what actually went on
in the lives of people who could not live otherwise than in the
circumstance to which they were bound. Also, since I was young

enough to feel the influence of my upbringing, I believed in the
Bible's assertion that words were not to be taken in vain. Since
God was the source of all life, as I had been taught, words were
not playthings. Williams fitted my ideal of the man who did not
take words in vain, neither as playthings nor as masks for one's
self-centeredness. In my fundamentalist approach to Stevens, his
use of words as playthings and masks were aberrations.

But I returned to his poems time and again because, in the
process of reading criticism and reviews, teaching myself the sub-
tleties and nuances of contemporary poetry, I found Stevens's
name coming up for discussion, now in praise, now in scathing
attack. Conflict was quite open and loud.

It will take a thorough self-examination to arrive at a full de-
scription of a nearly total turnabout from my earliest judgment of
Stevens. My self-examination must begin in the middle of the
Great Depression, with its concomitant griefs and angers. It will
embrace a territory even larger than the aesthetic because to me
Williams also meant the world of politics, society, work, relation-
ships with others and inevitably the kind of poetry that arose from
just such concerns of ordinary life. I was a newly married man,
the father of a son born to us in the midst of the Depression.
Where, I would ask myself, did Stevens come off, writing such
verbose poems of play and pretension to some kind of transcen-
dental apartness when the world was lying prostrate before a
berserk juggernaut of economics? Like millions of others, I was
caught up in its madness. Williams, as doctor, was witness to it
all in his writing and in his life, often overlooking and even re-
fusing the fee due him from indigent patients, consequently mak-
ing life for himself and his family a hardship. I felt more in com-
mon with him than with Stevens, and yet somehow I knew that
Stevens and Williams were, at the time, close friends. Although
Williams was critical of Stevens, sensing in Stevens a sensibility
diametrically opposite his own, he was admiring of just this dif-
ference between them, especially Stevens's way with words, no

matter that they depended more on persiflage than on the power
and exactness that Williams demanded of his own poems.

Were there two sides to Williams, I would ask myself. Was he
willing to acknowledge that Stevens could enter into his, Wil-
liams's, canon of achievement? Williams strove for meaning
through language that brought life to the page. Was this not what
was meant when one read that words were not to be taken in
vain, especially in life that was as hard, as deprived, and as dan-
gerously unpredictable as we were experiencing it then? Williams
puzzled me by his apparent double standard toward Stevens. Wor-
shipping the poet in the man, I was thrown back upon myself to
examine myself as the one who might be at fault in my attitude
toward Stevens.

I had my thinking to do, but I had living to do also. The aes-
thetic for me at the time was to save my sanity and my family and
pride. I must either learn to cope with life's slipperiness and im-
personalness, its sudden cruelties and disconnectedness, or else
sink beneath the fury of it all. I was creating an aesthetic, although
I did not realize it, that approached Stevens's own in principle with
the methods and vision learned from Williams.

I learned that Stevens was a lawyer. His early travels for the
Hartford Insurance Company took him to cities and towns where
he represented the insurance company in claims against it, gen-
erally settling them out of court but keeping always before him
the good of the company he represented and, as a not insignificant
by-product, his own good. He was, in effect, the ordinary man.
He could not have had illusions about that life. There could be
none in settling insurance claims. He was learning how to live
in this country, as I was.

Many years later, when I had published five books of poetry
and received several national awards and grants, I rested from
anxiety and aggressiveness. I could look back upon the voyage
I had undertaken, and survival was its name. I, too, like Stevens,
had had to confront the clash of interests, financial and personal,

to find my way past them with an energy and, when necessary, with a ruthlessness that disregarded consequences, all in behalf of my own well-being and that of the loved ones who depended on me. I, too, had had to cultivate the indifference and impersonalness that was in life itself, and, with some satisfaction, watch my antagonists in daily competition for work to supply the bindery go down to defeat. I could not empathize when my own life and welfare were at stake in confrontation with my competitors in business. Stevens never addressed this problem directly, yet despite the impersonal tone of most of his poems, it was clear where his thoughts lay:

United Dames of America

Je tâche, en restant
exact, d'être poète [*sic*]

There are not leaves enough to cover the face
It wears. This is the way the orator spoke:
"The mass is nothing. The number of men in a mass
Of men is nothing. The mass is no greater than

The singular man of the mass. Masses produce
Each one its paradigm." There are not leaves
Enough to hide away the face of the man
Of this dead mass and that. The wind might fill

With faces as with leaves, be gusty with mouths,
And with mouths crying and crying day by day.
Could all these be ourselves, sounding ourselves,
Our faces circling round a central face

And then nowhere again, away and away?
Yet one face keeps returning (never the one),
The face of the man of the mass, never the face
That hermit on reef sable would have seen,

Never the naked politician taught
By the wise. There are not leaves enough to crown,
To cover, to crown, to cover—let it go—
The actor that will at last declaim our end.

Competition, one-upmanship, was the deadly game in this country, and the sooner one learned it the quicker one became adept at it. I had learned it quickly. This, then, was what Stevens had gone through, as I was realizing, and perhaps still was going through in his promotion to executive vice-president of the Hartford Insurance Company. News of this kind travels fast among poets. It was exactly the experience of fierce combativeness of someone embattled that Williams was trying to capture in the poems with which I felt an affinity. This was his aesthetic, as it was mine. But Stevens?

Of course. What I had called his persiflage was his recreation, his withdrawal from the battle lines to recoup with distracting symbols and entertaining sounds. It was not that he was playing irresponsibly with meaning, which he took seriously, but rather that he had found meaning and language to be synonymous, even if fractured, tenuous, tentative.

Was the lesson Stevens derived from his struggle to survive as a lawyer one of combativeness and aggressiveness and was this consistent with the meaning to which he had been conditioned in his youth in his role as an obedient, affectionate son in a stable, orderly home, attending church, far removed from the struggle and tumult of the marketplace? There was love, and there was beauty, but these are not sufficient for existence, not in our country. I realized that Stevens was seeking, in wordplay, relief from his disillusionments, from the overwhelming evidence of the contradictions of meaning and value, as I was. In wordplay Stevens found the strength with which to speak his mind—through indirection. The French Symbolist poets played a role in his practice of oblique language.

I was seeking to go beyond that and other influences upon him to an understanding of the man himself. Temperament made the important difference between Williams and Stevens. Williams fought for the exact word and measure in conformity with the thing itself as he perceived it, in effect to possess it, control it, gain mastery of it, as though it was possible with words to master the life in which these things inhered. Stevens went in the opposite direction. In the absence of pleasure in existence he would write to entertain himself. He would make a world of sound and sense that would not only amuse and divert him but become a kind of existence he could enter into at any time the urge came to do so; it would be an existence to compensate what life itself had failed to do for him and what he had failed to do in life. From this play, he could derive both love and pleasure, a certain orderliness and stability. The love would reflect back upon him from the love he would pour into his pleasure with words, the same pleasure that would apply to meaning, to order and stability.

And so in Stevens I became aware of a personality totally unlike mine in motivation and practice, such as I had never before met in American poetry. There was Mallarmé, whom I read with intense interest. In Mallarmé I could see a temperament much like Stevens's and one Stevens admired. I began to understand Williams's interest and rivalrous friendship with Stevens and Stevens's reciprocation in kind. Williams, too, had studied the French poets and had attempted translations and exercises in their modes: Dadaism and Surrealism, as in *Kora in Hell*. Stevens was attracted to certain of Williams's poems; he appropriated several of Williams's titles and lines to reply to the poems themselves, intending to place the emphasis of those titles and lines within his own sense of things. Here were two men who had lost their innocence about America long ago; each could recognize in the other the loss, with a certain respect for the other's special kind of loss.

I have not yet touched upon the crucial likeness between them. Williams was apparently the hard literalist. Stevens was airy, self-enraptured. Where, then, were they joined in the uses of the imagination? Does it matter that one person sees the world plainly, as if it were before him in its nakedness, needing only to be transcribed to appear on the page as naked as in life, while another person sees life as the signs and portents of another existence, in himself or in the world or beyond the world? Are there two forms of the imagination or only one, and that one of symbols and signs? According to the second theory, to imagine is to conceive of what is not, while according to the first theory, that which already is is the imagination already before us, the world conceived by divine or mysterious force, the function of the artist or, for that matter anyone, being to accept it as it is. Can anyone accept what is before him or her as it is? Has anyone such an ability? Will two persons testify with the same faithfulness to detail and meaning about an incident both have experienced at the same time and place? Of course not. Is this the imagination at work, or should we call it temperament, distortion, or perspective? What does it matter what we call it? It is still the imagination at work, the conceiving apparatus in each of us and peculiar to each of us. Since that is so, to criticize and reject Williams as a literalist is meaningless, for he conceives the world as he experiences it from the totality of his lifestand. Stevens too acknowledged over and over that grass grows, that buildings stand, that people walk, talk, make love, kill, eat, sleep, defecate, quarrel, and debate. What happens when each of us begins to talk or write about these things? We know what happens. Whose reality, we may ask, do we believe in? Whose imagination?

On the other hand, some will say that the imagination is utterly removed from these infinitely varied perceptions, as with Stevens, who seemed to draw upon a world distinctly and uniquely his own, removing himself from the reality he perceived, except to touch base before departing from it. This is not so far removed from Williams's stand. In "Paterson," he writes,

> Without invention nothing is well spaced,
> unless the mind change, unless
> the stares are new measured, according
> to their relative positions, the
> line will not change, the necessity
> will not matriculate: unless there is
> a new mind there cannot be a new
> line, the old will go on
> repeating itself with recurring
> deadliness: without invention
> nothing lies under the witch-hazel
> bush, the alder does not grow from among

    the hummocks margining the all
    .but spent channel of the old swale,
    the small foot-prints
    of the mice under the overhanging
    tufts of the bunch-grass will not
    appear: without invention the line
    will never again take on its ancient
    divisions when the word, a supple word,
    lived in it, crumbled now to chalk.

And from "Notes Towards a Supreme Fiction,"

I

    Begin, ephebe, by perceiving the idea
    Of this invention, this invented world,
    The inconceivable idea of the sun.

    You must become an ignorant man again
    And see the sun again with an ignorant eye
    And see it clearly in the idea of it.

    Never suppose an inventing mind as source
    Of this idea nor for that mind compose
    A voluminous master folded in his fire.

    How clean the sun when seen in its idea,
    Washed in the remotest cleanliness of a heaven
    That has expelled us and our images. . . .

    The death of one god is the death of all.
    Let purple Phoebus lie in umber harvest,
    Let Phoebus slumber and die in autumn umber,

    Phoebus is dead, ephebe. But Phoebus was
    A name for something that never could be named
    There was a project for the sun and is.

    There is a project for the sun. The sun
    Must bear no name, gold flourisher, but be
    In the difficulty of what it is to be.

    While Stevens takes a tragic view of change and re-creation in the mind and purpose of humankind, Williams, with images close to and of the earth, affirms the necessity for change in tones of determination and of the earth itself. Temperament separates them, yet in thought, in point of view, in purpose, they are completely aligned. I anticipate that some will claim that Stevens and Williams are using the word *invention* with different meanings. But that is the point. Whose meaning do we want to accept? But why should we not accept both? I came across a book by David Walker on exactly this issue, *The Transparent Lyric*. The subtitle is "Reading and Meaning in the Poetry of Stevens and Williams." In it, Walker writes "By frankly acknowledging its own status as a fiction, a deliberate construction, the work of art could attain a liberating vitality and immediacy. William Carlos Williams and Wallace Stevens were among the first to recognize the literary application of this principle."

I can offer statements by Stevens that are in direct accord with this statement by David Walker, and I will, but first let me summarize what I wish to underscore in treating these two poets as equals of one another, as complementary opposites who were, after everything is said, dealing each with a difference in emphasis, not in contradiction of one another. For Stevens, the use of imagining was itself the reality. For Williams, it was what imagination brought forth from among the facts of living. To put it yet another way, Stevens looked to the imagination for the poetry of life. Williams looked at imagination or invention, as both he and Stevens spoke and wrote about it, for its power to inspire love of the object as transformed by the imagination. Who, in any position, is wise enough to make a distinction of superiority between these two modes of perception? In the collection of essays *The Necessary Angel,* Stevens wrote "for one thing, the great poems of heaven and hell have been written and the great poem of the earth remains to be written." This fits in and is in accord with Williams's practice as poet. And so to make distinctions of superiority between the two modes of the imagination as practiced by Williams and Stevens, as though they were in opposition to one another, which they are not, is to miss the yet more significant point. The so-called literalist of the imagination and his supposed opposite, the purist of the imagination, create a whole of aesthetic delight in reinforcing one another in the wrting of the poem. If one is not yet convinced of this organic and symbiotic relationship, there is another statement from Stevens, from *Imagination as Value:* "It is not that the imagination is versatile but that there are different imaginations."

That Stevens found it necessary to write as if the world hung before him in a mist of which he had to make it a world he could inhabit imaginatively and possess is no different in principle from that of Williams who found the world lying before him in the gutter, that is, in that famous brown sheet of rumpled paper rolling in the wind to be crushed under a car wheel, only to right itself and keep on rolling in the wind. The difference between these two poets some will call sensibility. If Stevens must see the world in a mist of propositions about the world of which he must make a construct of words, Williams perceives life as struggle, the outcome uncertain, between forces of which he must make a world that can survive the conflict. Both poets are stating the same proposition, that the world exists for each to make something of it in order to live in harmony with the self through his poetry about the world, this despite the differences from the reality of the poem.

Critics have found Stevens the superior poet in style and thought, a distinction in Stevens's case nearly impossible to make. In theme and subject, I have found both poets strikingly alike, the difference between them being their treatment of these themes and subjects For both, life was bleak and unpromising, but for both the imagination could lift this bleakness to a level of awareness so that in the poem it became another thing, apart from the world. Each could invest it with his temperament or sensibility or his passion to make it his own, to possess a mastery that is the joy, self-awareness, pride, and balance between life and death.

I know there is more yet to be said. I know of the variousness of style in Williams, independent of the poetry of social commentary that helped shape my own aesthetic. I know of the deep changes in style in Stevens with the years, toward gravity and plainness, in a way that resembles the later Williams.

I have learned to live with both poets on an equable basis, my love of poetry equally divided between their modes with, of course, certain fine distinctions. I have spoken as fully as I am able of a complex, troubled controversy, hoping it will help bring the theme of reconciliation and belated recognition to the forefront of discussion on a much wider and more fundamental basis.

Perhaps I have written the prose poem of reconciliation between the two primary complementary poetic voices in American poetry, or alternately, "American society," a bifurcated culture. I believe in the integrated relationship between poetry and society. To me, Williams and Stevens are representative of this divided American culture and thus continue to be bound together indissolubly, functioning as the figurative opposites they are. Stevens remained coolly apart from the issues that torment our society, though he was perfectly aware of them, while Williams permitted this social torment into his poems, letting it shape his aesthetic in significant ways. It is a terrible error for certain critics to isolate these two poets from each other as poets, to remove Stevens from the social context in which he lived and wrote, creating a desert around him and placing him on a dusty throne. It is a tragic distortion of the history these two men lived together. As David Walker writes, "Stevens and Williams were the two poets of their generation most influenced by the new art movements determined to break the mold of fixed perspective and to make art actual and immediate by eliciting the reader's vital imagination." Each succeeded in his way to the fullest.

We are today witness to a clash in the academy and among the poets between the adherents of Williams, in the evident minority, and the adherents of Stevens, the majority. It is a clash that would have raised their eyebrows in amusement, if not in amazement, for both respected and recognized the contribution of aesthetic principle held in common between them—of the ground each held to plow and seed. Ignoring this truth, American poetry, I believe, is suffering a deepening division and, as a consequence, losing that vitality that springs from respectful rivalry. Authorities on Stevens are riding high over the body of Williams's work, as if seeking to trample it into oblivion. If they were to succeed poetry would stand an arid field for generations to come.

Neither Williams nor Stevens could anticipate this ugly domination by one or the other. Neither would have opted for domination. One has only to read their letters and their essays, which at times explicitly, at other times implicitly, state that it will take mutual understanding to create a climate of a meaningful and respectful contest, one that would give the poet a role in the making of a spirit of community within an enlivened, broadened national culture.

Surely Stevens would have scorned to see his poems turned into ammunition with which to shoot down other poets. We see a nearly military discipline around the corpus Stevens and with a kind of devastation in the immediate area. We miss the spirit of Stevens, his playfulness, his pleasure in the arts, his perseverance in the face of the ridicule he had to endure. Let us recall his debt to imagination with which a poet strengthens his resolve to work at his own unique practice. It seems to me that Stevens would have wanted to join with Williams in applauding such a resolve. He too had been lonely and isolated, as had Williams, in his early days. The two stand together, encouraging us to carry on in the tradition of perseverance to which each contributed with courage and joy in the work itself. A poem by Williams, "Convivio," best sums it up:

> We forget sometimes that no matter what
> our quarrels we are the same brotherhood:
> the rain falling or the rain withheld,
> —berated by women, barroom smells
> or breath of Persian roses! our wealth
> is words. And when we go down to defeat,
> before the words, it is still within and
> the concern of, first, the brotherhood.
> Which should quiet us, warm and arm us
> besides to attack, always attack—but to
> reserve our worst blows for the enemy, those

who despise the word, flout it, stem,
leaves and root; the liars who decree laws
with no purpose other than to make a screen
of them for larceny, murder—for our
murder, we who salute the word and would
have it clean, full of sharp movement.

11. Robert Bly

I first met Robert Bly by telephone, either at my apartment or at the bindery where I was employed; but I am inclined to believe that I received the call at home because I was in a relaxed state. It was sometime in the late fifties. Robert's was a voice that I had never before heard, strong, as if exulting in its strength, a voice in joy of itself that seemed to carry a message of some extraordinary dispensation toward others, particularly the one being addressed at that moment. I was all attention. He had demanded to know whether I was David Ignatow. After my reply, his voice dropped a full octave to begin speaking confidentially, identifying itself as the voice of Robert Bly. Had I heard of him, it asked. I had to confess I had not. The voice went on, and here I can only paraphrase his remarks which, in brief, spoke of his admiration for my poems. Out of nowhere, it seemed, had come a voice to give me heart again, to set me up in my own eyes as poet.

It is difficult to remember what followed between us, but as I sit here typing it comes back to me that I probably next visited him at his apartment in Greenwich Village. I had taken time off from my demanding routine at the bindery, just enough time in which to pay a courtesy call in return for his phone call. The pressure on me to return to work that afternoon was strong, as usual, much as I was filled with guilt for having told my father, the boss, that I had urgent shop business on the outside. I remember sitting with Robert in his apartment, but I do not remember in detail what we talked about. I would think it had to be about poetry and, if my fading memory can be relied on, he did ask me about the circumstances under which I made my living. About that I was always self-conscious—a poet working in a bindery shop. It didn't accord with the conventional version of a poet seated in a cafe over a glass of wine with his fellow poets or seated in a locked room bare of furniture, except for a desk, a bed, and a table. Robert himself didn't seem to fit that conventional mode either, so the self-consciousness I felt about describing my way of making a living was eased by his warm, sympathetic, and even admiring manner. When finally I left, having to excuse myself on account of business—I was angry at myself for having to say it and angry at the job that forced me to leave—I resolved to learn more about his poetry.

I had recognized an out-of-towner, a midwesterner by his demeanor and accent. In fact, first speaking to him by phone the week before, I had vaguely sensed this from his diction and speech tones, and so as he spoke I became doubly admiring of him for having the insight and empathy to feel and know city poetry, the kind I was writing then. I was amazed at his pleasure in city themes—this from a midwesterner who I sensed was of the wide-open spaces, miles from urban life, a man who had probably grown up amid fields of corn, wheat, barley, and rye, amid horses and wild flowing grasses that stretched toward the horizon.

Apparently, as I came to realize, Robert had called me on the phone after the publication in 1957 of *New Poets of England and America,* edited by Louis Simpson, Donald Hall, and Robert Pack. It was an anthology dedicated to a new mode of poetry. Robert's poems there, when I read them after our first meeting, seemed traditional both in rhyme and stanzaic forms. Well done, yes, but disappointing by comparison with Robert's strong, uplifting sense of himself as poet and as missionary to the poets, which had come across to me during our first visit together. That he should have spent my brief visit with him in his apartment praising my work and speaking with such interest—curiosity would be more appropriate—about my life and conditions and my vision of the city—all this had prepared me for a different kind of poetry. And so I suspected he was in the midst of an inner struggle or conflict. I had to remember that I had consciously chosen to take the road opposite his and that I had persisted in it and was persisting in it defiantly in the face of opprobrium of the then established poets. Already I had published two volumes, both at my expense, the first, *Poems,* in 1948, the second in 1955. The second, *The Gentle Weight Lifter,* was influenced by the poetry of William Carlos Williams. I suspected that Robert was undergoing a conversion of spirit, while learning to understand and appreciate the virtues of the principles of freely organized form, and I suspected that he was having a difficult time of it as a conventionally trained midwestern poet living in the uproar and violence of New York City. Perhaps, the thought occurred to me, I was his cicerone in his journey toward the then forbidden and denigrated, if not totally despised, principles of free form. Had he, living in New York, come to see that these principles were precisely what fit poetry that tried to communicate city life? These were my thoughts after meeting with him that afternoon.

Thereafter, we met infrequently. I really can't recall our next city meeting, but I do remember Carol Bly's coming to visit me in the shop shortly afterward. Why Robert was not with her I never thought of asking, but to see her coming to my place of business was, to me, at first an awkward surprise, since I too was in conflict with myself about the course I had taken in poetry, isolated as I was from the "kingly" realm of rhyme and meter. Carol had come to watch me at work, to view the proficiency with which I managed the workers at their machines, the speed and effectiveness with which I answered the phones and wrote out orders for scheduled jobs. Listening to her compliments, I began to feel proud of my occupational skills. After all, I was doing the anti-poetic thing poetry needed for vitality, and I was being admired for it. As Carol finally left, after walking slowly through the shop turning her head this way and that to catch the rhythms, tensions, and sounds of the machines and their workers, I knew I had made a new and solid friendship based on, of all things, my work in the bindery which, to confess, until that moment I had hated and despaired of ever leaving. It was a paradox to me but

an exciting one suddenly, and I had Carol and Robert to thank
for this new view I could have of myself. I was not alone in my
commitment to the daily life of most men and women at work
in factories and offices and behind sales counters. I was not alone
in dedicating my poetry to writing about this ordinariness. Robert's
and Carol's introduction to and esteem for my life made it a
triumph of vindication for me who had had secret doubts about
my efforts to portray in poetry the people I knew, the conditions
I lived in, the life I had to live.

Now I remember one more meeting in Robert's apartment, and
it had to do with one of James Wright's most famous and beau-
tiful poems, "Lying in a Hammock at William Duffy's Farm in
Pine Island." Robert let me see it in manuscript, which he had
gotten from Jim by mail, I believe—Jim was then teaching at the
University of Minnesota. I was astonished, flabbergasted by the
last line, "I have wasted my life"—this after the superb description
of such beauty that I could not equate that last line with what
came before it. I thought of the last line as a complete anomaly,
an aberration, a total misunderstanding and misrepresentation of
himself, the poet who could write with surpassing beauty, but
Robert smiled at my excited disagreement. He understood some-
thing more. He argued with me gently. I argued passionately that
the marvelous lines that came before that last one gave the lie
to Jim's statement of a wasted life. How could a poet think of
having wasted his life when those lines showed exactly the oppo-
site, an achievement of such great strength and love of life and
its details. Robert argued calmly that the point was not the beauty
of those lines but the insight into the order and calm lives of
others, a calm and order that was their achievement, of which Jim
had nothing to compare in his life that this last line revealed. I'm
afraid it took me several years to absorb that insight; eventually
I did, but not before undergoing, in my way, experiences such as
Jim had gone through. This was no ordinary run of the mill mid-
westerner, Robert Bly, who had argued gently with me for his
understanding of the poem. Robert had been there ahead of me.

He had hold of something I then did not know or was not then fully conscious of in myself, despite my dark poems of city life. I had not yet faced the fact that life in the city was in itself a waste, as lived in shops, factories, offices. Though I knew of it in others, I who was writing the poems, the successful poems, had not been prepared to know it in my own life. Jim had been confronting himself on this issue in his particular circumstances and Robert had known it.

At that time and perhaps at that very same meeting I got to read Robert's city poems, his attempt at recording the city from his standpoint as a midwesterner. I was not so much impressed with as respectful of his effort. Except for one or two poems, I thought something of the city rhythms and tone was missing. There was too much of the prophetic voice, precisely what could not apostrophize nor perhaps hope to reform a city that by its very nature ran on strict concern with money, with pleasures derived from money, with rewards derived from money, a life-style in itself that lived by money and was the city's existence; in sum, a kind of managed disorder and violence that flowed from precisely this drive in each individual: anarchic for its emphasis upon the person to the exclusion of the city as a living whole. Who, then, of the city would assume that the city could be laid low with a prophetic blast, such a city of stone and heedless traffic? In brief, Robert's poems lacked the insider's view of it: the sarcasm, the weariness with money, with pleasures made paltry with excess of them, the scorn of oneself and of others caught up in and enthusiastically pursuing spiritual desuetude. I could praise several of his poems, those that caught the outsider's wonder about the disorder in adults who could raise their violent, unhappy voices at night when the outsider, as a midwesterner, could remember only the silence and peace of the open fields and night sky.

Then Robert left for home, and I was to hear from him again through the receipt of his first volume of poems, *Silence in the Snowy Fields,* in 1962. I knew I held in my hand a masterpiece of midwestern sensibility. Nothing in it moved me so much as that sense of awe of his environment, the order and beauty he found in it. I knew I was in the presence of a spirit unique to the American experience in the Midwest, something I had never before encountered, and I became aware of a different America from what I had come to think was the one and only kind, the city.

Robert eventually accepted two poems of mine on two separate occasions for two separate issues of the magazine *The Sixties*. The first poem, if I'm not mistaken, was "The Dream." A man is pounding his head on the sidewalk in front of a department store in a huge city, a nightmare poem of city life. Robert saw it for what it meant; he could see clear through to the actual event as a true city poem. But the next poem he accepted had been written under the spell of his *Silence in the Snowy Fields*. I had admired the book so much, I was envious of the beauty and rest, calm and faith he had found in his surroundings, and I was made to realize I was ignoring my own experience. It had been something I had yearned for and loved in my adolescence when I had lived in the spacious suburbs that were then Brooklyn, its open fields, its trees, its silent night sky, the summer evening of fireflies, and the long leisurely walks across the fields with friends. All this I had bitterly left behind me to merge with the city to earn my living from it. I sent Robert a poem that was partly a salute to him, in remembrance of my own lost paradise that yet in memory was real to me, as real as was Robert actually living in the Midwest. The poem, "Earth Hard," was very brief. Robert accepted it and let me know that, master of natural description and response that he was, he had found my poem authentic. It set me off to write in that vein again and again; I was thrilled to have recovered that part of me out of the muck and fury of city life, not that I was through with writing about the city, but I had this past to balance it with and to help me keep my balance at last.

The Vietnam War that followed this euphoric period was the climactic experience for us both in the sixties, but Robert did something about its frightening face and form, its horrific insanity. Almost singlehandedly, he launched a campaign of speeches, demonstrations, readings and read-ins, and poem writing across the college campuses of the nation. He withheld paying his taxes as yet another form of personal resistance to the war and published *The Light Around the Body,* a complete turnaround from *Silence in the Snowy Fields. The Light Around the Body* was a statement of national anguish, of the sense of national betrayal by those in power, drunk and arrogant with power. The book won the coveted and then highly respected National Book Award. I for one was already electrified by Robert's heroic fight in the latter half of the sixties. I joined him and Galway Kinnell in a car trip to Harvard University where we read each from our antiwar poems to a packed audience of students and faculty members. A year or so earlier, with Robert as an inspiration, I had gathered my courage to participate in a protest march down the main street of Lawrence, Kansas, where I was then teaching at the university. It was at least four years since I had given up the bindery at my father's death. At the protest march, we were photographed every step of the way by persons who were probably FBI agents and local detectives. On our return to campus where we sat down in front of the administration building, we were threatened by the savage expressions of hatred of youths in expensive Oldsmobiles and Cadillacs. There were cops there too who carried their sidearms openly and came to look down on us impassively, as if we were objects for inspection and disposal in some form at their discretion. We knew the Vietnam savagery was there upon us, but we sat the scheduled time.

The Light Around the Body brought Robert the National Book Award when I was back from Kansas and teaching at Vassar. I and all his friends knew that accepting the prize in front of a huge audience, as was the custom, would give Robert a superb opportunity to speak out against the war. To Robert, at first, the idea of accepting a prize in the middle of a war of devastation upon innocent people was obscene and a travesty of the high purpose of poetry itself. He was for rejecting the prize outright with a written, scathing denunciation, but talking this out with

Paul Zweig, James Wright, and me, as I remember, he decided
finally to accept the award on condition that he be allowed to
speak as he wished. It was an unusual request to make to the
committee, since it was the custom then simply to accept the prize
with a short but graceful thank you and depart from the stage.
However, the climate of the times being what it was, and Robert's
passionate efforts against the war being already known, permission
was reluctantly granted, and Paul, Jim, Saul Galin, and I sat down
to rewrite a speech that Robert had begun. After reading through
what he had written so far, we realized, as Robert came to realize
in discussions with him, that the speech had to be written in a
measured and calm rhetoric to be the more convincing to the
august atmosphere of the occasion. The speech finally was written
among us just hours before the ceremony was to start, and it was
an amazing moment in the hall when Robert, after quietly re-
ceiving the check, turned to the audience with his speech in hand
and began to read it in his measured but angry voice. He de-
nounced the war, those who had begun it and were pursuing it;
he denounced the writers in the audience who had been sitting by
idly, letting the war take its frightful course without a word of
protest or expression of conscience; and, finally, he denounced
the publishers themselves who had contributed toward the prize
money, and his own publisher in particular, for their silence dur-
ing the war in the face of its overwhelming significance as an on-
slaught upon the liberty and civil rights of an entire nation. This
significance could by extension be applied to the developing con-
dition in this country in which publishing itself could be threat-
ened by governmental censorship and intimidation. It was a fact
that was already being felt in the publishing world without a word
of protest from anyone in the field. Robert ended by accepting the
check with the sole intention of then and there handing it to a
representative of the War Resister's League who would receive
it for use in helping to resist the war in whatever manner the
League saw fit. A hush fell upon the audience as Robert called
out the name of the representative to come to the platform to

receive the check. As the check passed between them, Robert offered him a final admonishment—to refuse to register for the draft upon his, Robert's, urging. Such a refusal and the open encouragement of such a refusal amounted to a violation of a law that had recently been passed in Congress. There was silence in the hall for a moment, the silence of extreme tension until, finally, a small scattering of handclapping began. We had been forewarned that there would be FBI agents in the audience, and as we looked around we became aware that about ten men dressed in dark suits rose up from their seats in different parts of the hall and walked out in a body. The rest of the audience now had begun an uproar of talk mixed with boos and cheers. The die had been cast for Robert and for us. We had thrown down the challenge to the government. I was apprehensive that the worst was yet to come, but who at that moment would let that fear override the exhilaration, that victory of spirit that swept through us who had helped Robert with his speech? We knew that whatever government reprisal might follow, we could deal with it as it happened. For now we had won the day and put on notice the government and this distinguished audience, composed of most of the major literary figures of the time and their publishers, that this war could not be suppressed in our thoughts, nor in our lives, but had to be met honestly and with conscience. Donald Hall and Ted Weiss, two of the three judges who had given Robert his prize, were also seated in the audience.* Although they were keeping their own counsel, we knew very well what had motivated their decision. And so, for me the moment meant a complete and overwhelming affirmation and vindication of all that Robert stood for as a crusading, visionary figure in the literary world and in the politics of the nation. He had endured insults, threats, and condemnation to make his stand before the artistic and intellectual elite at the full height of his career and poetic talents. He was a man for all seasons. He had done it with all the style, gusto, and

* Editor's note: Harvey Shapiro, the third judge, was in Europe at the time of the awards ceremony.

political passion on the highest level. It was Robert's finest hour, and we who were attached to him through admiration, faith, and common goals were affirmed through him and made to feel our significance before the world.

For the present, I would prefer that others, with their versions, continue this account of Robert's fortunes as poet, man, and crusader, but this much I can state in conclusion. Robert is a man in change, growing deeper into himself and into the consciousness of his readers and audience, precisely because of his deepening life and new ways of writing it. Much already is emerging in his poems and in his choice of poets to translate that is significant for an understanding of where he is headed as poet. I am willing to state here that he has only now begun to see the outlines of his future as poet and that, as I see it, that future is extraordinary and of central importance to American writing yet to come.

12. Paul Blackburn

It was Paul Blackburn's elegant nonchalance that first attracted me. Among poets with whom I was associating at the time, most of us were either being harassed by debts, jobs, domesticity, or writer's block. Paul had the air of a man who knew his way around these potholes with a casual grace, while hanging his cigarette from a corner of his mouth and holding forth on his beloved Provençal poets. I would listen, fascinated but intensely puzzled. How, I had to ask myself, had he become so deeply attached to poets who were not known or even heard of, let alone whose language no longer was being spoken or written? But that Paul was this totally taken up, his whole being centered upon it—he could at a moment's notice quote any number of lines from Arnaut Daniel or any of the Provençal poets—made it a reality for me that he and these mysterious poets with their strange charm were one and the same being, as if Paul had come down the centuries to be with us and to teach us the beauty, sweetness, and raciness of the spirit of those long-ago years. Its contrast with what most of us were experiencing in our strained contemporary lives was shocking, but also deeply challenging, and Paul was the spirit who led us through to a recognition of what was missing in our lives.

One of the last days of my closeness to him happened here in East Hampton where I live. We sat on the beach facing the Atlantic Ocean. Paul was there, and his wife and child. I watched him light cigarette after cigarette, worried about him, disturbed that he persisted in smoking despite warnings from his doctor, as he was to tell me casually in reply to my polite enquiry. He already was having difficulty swallowing his food. His behavior was to me unsettling. It was in direct contradiction to what he stood for among us, an animating spirit in our lives. Bitterly, it was as if that nonchalance of spirit toward worldly concerns was taking him to his death.

I saw him off the following day with his family. They were on their way to his new teaching job at Cortlandt College, a position given to him in recognition of what he already had achieved in his own poems and in translations from the Provencal. He had been appointed as poet-in-residence, and we looked to the day when he would be calling on us to come and read from our own work in his role there as director of readings by visiting poets. Yet as I saw him off, I could not but be aware of a foreboding, after having heard him cough harshly and, it seemed to me, pain-fully, and after having observed him gently pushing away his breakfast when it became difficult for him to swallow what he had chewed. He is gone, but we still find him among us as man and poet in our enduring memories of him. He was kind and gracious to those of us who were just starting out as practicing poets. Paul had directed a reading series at the Deux Magots on 2nd Avenue, where he would go out of his way to invite unknown poets to come and read, while he taped them for posterity.

Typically, he treated his own literary problems factually, as if they were simply problems in the mechanics of publication. It helped shield him from his frustrations, that which we all shared in our experience of submitting manuscripts for publication. Most of us would exclaim in disgust and anger at rejections. Paul would brush off his own failures with a sharp, sardonic witticism or a colorful obscenity directed at the publisher, and then proceed energetically to the next matter at hand.

I had the pleasure, as manager of my father's book bindery, of accepting page proofs and cover for a chapbook by Paul, titled *The Nets,* to be folded, collated, stitched and trimmed, and packed for distribution. I did it all free of charge with delight. Jerry Rothenberg and Armand Schwerner, if I remember accurately, had hauled the sheets and covers by pushcart from the printers and waited around with me in my office as the sheets were being folded into pages. The year may have been 1961.

There are poems of Paul's—"Gathering Winter Fuel" and "Clickety Clack," to name two—that are here to stay. They are evocations of a spirit with which all of us can identify in its truth to circumstance, in its passion for the exact word, and in the beauty of its tolerance for life. That last may sound strange, but in that phrase I hear reverberations of his love for the whole wide spectrum of life that he found in the writings of the Provençals—sometimes hilarious, at times outright brutal, more often lovely with the charm of exotic conditions and circumstances within those poems. Perhaps he had learned tolerance from the long, exhausting work of translation and revision, over and over. Perhaps he had learned to endure, to become one of the troubadours in the depth of his affection for them. Where else, I have asked myself, did he learn to affect that elegant nonchalance of his but from his wide-ranging sympathies and acceptance, as would come from dedicated commitment to the otherworldly Provençals. Nonchalance he equated with tolerance. Perhaps it was how he learned to tolerate his own death, with the nonchalance that all was acceptable. Perhaps it was his greatest triumph, to accept death in his tolerance for its role in life. It could explain to me his casual reply to my question on the beach about his condition. Here could be the answer to my then worried thoughts, and if I have found the answer to be true, at least as I believe it is, then to bid him farewell is to do so in recognition that he had lived his life to the fullest of which he was capable and that it was for us to memorialize and to celebrate the life of a fulfilled man and poet.

13. Wendell Berry

One Sunday morning in 1966, Wendell Berry called me up from Kentucky to ask me to substitute for him at the University of Kentucky. He had just received his Rockefeller Foundation grant. It was about a year since Wendell and I met in New York at a reading by Auden. After the reading, Wendell and I got to talking with each other, and as we were walking together down the street I said that it would be nice to look back on New York from a distance of a thousand miles. Wendell had just finished telling me that he was about to return to Kentucky, his teaching stint at NYU being completed. At that time, I hadn't been farther from New York than Hoboken, and the thought of putting distance between me and the city was appealing. I loved the city, but it was tiring me out with pressures of many years. Yet my first response to Wendell's invitation was, to my own astonishment, a flat no. Wendell was shocked into silence. Suddenly, the thought of my leaving the city had panicked me, exactly as it would have panicked a small town inhabitant to be told he had to leave his familiar, assured environment. As I hung up, knowing how disappointed Wendell felt, I was sorry for myself for being such an absurdly parochial character, and I had to admire Wendell for remembering our conversation and for acting on it. He was no provincial like myself. He would let me take his place at the University of Kentucky, where at that time New Yorkers were considered to be suspect. Wendell was absolutely willing to face that issue. In fact, it never intruded in his consciousness during our conversation. Wendell was the cosmopolitan, not I. It was I who had failed my upbringing and culture. With some prodding from my wife and from my friend and confidant, Milton Hindus, then teaching at Brandeis, now ashamed of myself, I called Wendell back the next day and accepted his offer.

What followed from that was, of course, significant for me personally, but if my stay in Kentucky did one thing, it opened up to me a wholly new vision of the country, and for this I have Wendell to thank. This experience with Wendell, for me, finds itself reflected in the roots and character of his poems. While Wendell Berry is profoundly attached to the soil and to his place of living, Port Royal, a farming community from which he draws his basic attitudes and life-style, his roots aesthetically are deep in the thinking and work of poets like William Carlos Williams. The unique quality of his poetry, which sets him apart from most other followers of Williams, is that he is vitally committed to one of Williams's principal precepts for the writing of the authentic poem, and that is the sense of place by which a poem is formed.

Reading Wendell's poems, we are immediately struck by the tone of deliberate conscious force, the kind of deliberation that goes into his farming, of that sense of ritual and ceremony, the significance of which expresses itself in the acts of seeding, maturation, and harvesting. It is this experience that informs the very pace and diction of his poems and that radiates in Wendell's poetic vision of human redemption through identity with the life processes of which the working of the soil has made Wendell Berry awesomely aware. This is writing in the tradition of the Whitman of that marvelous poem "The Compost," in which life and death, health and disease, are finally resolved in the beneficence of the soil.

Whether he writes of love and family life or of social and political woes of the nation, Wendell's work is all of a piece, informed and taking its cue from the vision of humanity within the goodness of its first natural state before the onslaught of the industrial, technological age.

Wendell has published ten volumes of poetry as well as novels and nonfiction books, one of them dealing with slavery in the South,

tales handed down to him by his Kentucky ancestors. If anything
further should be said in praise of his poetry, it is that while he
is dedicated to his way of life, it is not without his keen perception
of the times in which we live as he maintains an organic relation-
ship with nature, the model of an upright man.

14. Charles Reznikoff

Those poems of Charles Reznikoff's I admired in the past still remain for me the best of his work—his marvelous Imagist and Objectivist poems, some not more than five lines long. In these modes he ranks with the masters of Chinese poetry, in my opinion. Reznikoff was writing about the immigrant working class mainly during the period when Carl Sandburg was flourishing as a poet of the people and gaining a worldwide reputation, but one has only to compare the work of these two poets to recognize the injustice done to Reznikoff by the silence critics let fall upon his books time after time as they emerged. If his style is calm and seemingly quiescent by comparison with Sandburg's exclamatory manner, Reznikoff is more tellingly precise and ultimately, as one reads poem after poem, far more profoundly illuminating.

Perhaps one explanation for the neglect with which he was treated during his lifetime could be found in his principles as a poet. Of them all, the principle which he practiced most faithfully and that shaped his best long poems derived from the Objectivist ideal to record events, situations, and even character studies with strictest adherence to the facts of the subject so that they could stand free, as it were, of the writer's overt arrangement. The facts were to speak for themselves, with the author merely arranging them in an order that would allow them to speak. It was a method designed to bring a greater influence to bear upon the reader, who would not feel the author intruding to voice his own judgments, thus permitting the reader to feel and appreciate the situation in its "pure" state. In one respect, the method could be likened to the role of court stenographers or of journalists who in conforming to the strict code of their professions must leave themselves out of the record entirely. But the truth of the matter, for Reznikoff, was that in letting the facts appear to stand freely on the page he believed he could accomplish that much more swiftly and deeply his purpose of alleviating the agonies of the people of his poems through the social reforms that he envisioned could be helped to birth through his poems' impact on the moral sensibilities of his readers. Reznikoff was a passionate moralist but also an artist in control. In short, he was a poet of the classical tradition, and blessed with great gifts.

Simply to read those poems that he wrote during the first quarter of this century and later is to recognize how true they are for today when the struggle still goes on among minorities to attain some reasonable integration with society against the heaviest odds. In the meanwhile, the poets of these minorities still take a back seat and are infrequently commented on in the press or given the opportunity to read or speak before the large mixed audiences that are enjoyed by other poets. Things haven't changed as much as they should.

Reznikoff wrote many different kinds of poems, in different styles and on a variety of subjects other than poverty, neglect, and suicide. He loved life intensely and wrote some of our most beautiful lyrics of city walking and observing. He was Jewish to the core, albeit an agnostic, and wrote poems passionately and directly on Jewish history past and present. He could also be philosophically worldly and these poems are among his finest.

Milton Hindus's study of Charles Reznikoff, a monograph of sixty-seven pages, closely thought through and documented, should be read as the authoritative statement on Reznikoff. Hindus was an intimate of Reznikoff and writes from long acquaintance with the work and man. The study, both biographical and critical, covers every important literary aspect and development, as well as everything of biographical significance related to his work. It is the key to the appreciation of the greatly talented, gentle being who once

walked among us without fanfare or hullabaloo, living his ordi-
nary routine existence in tranquility so as to leave us the gift of his
works, at his death, out of love and pity for us all.

I first met Charles Reznikoff in absentia through a conversation
with Louis Zukofsky at his house where I had had dinner and was
listening to Louis tell of his close friends, in particular Charles,
about whom I knew nothing at that time. Louis was urging me to
read Charles's poems, which, he believed, had an affinity with
mine. I listened with interest, as yet not persuaded since, after all,
I had not read his poems and actually had not heard of him before.
I was in a rather snobbish mood at the time. To have to hear that
Charles came of a poor, struggling family and was himself strug-
gling, having to publish his own books and, of course, in the na-
ture of that sort of publication, being neglected and overlooked—
all this made me rather self-conscious about my own circumstances.
I too had published my first volume at my own expense and with a
little money from my amused and tolerant father and I, too, was
struggling to find time to write after spending my days at hard
manual labor in factories. It made me all too uncomfortable to
have to hear that there was another like me in the same circum-
stances who was also being overlooked and neglected, except by
one or two close friends. Still, I listened to Louis, whose opinions I
deeply respected and whose poems I held in awe for their precision
and strength of line. And I promised to look up Charles's work at
the first opportunity.

Did I, though? It's a question that I can't answer truthfully
either way, and I'm prone to think that I decided not to at that
time because, after all, Charles and I had so much in common,
why bother to look at a mirror image? I was out for bigger things
than that. I was out for fame, fortune, love, and power. I was typi-
cal of the frustrated, deprived member of the lower middle class
with instincts toward accomplishment in the great, big, shining,
unattainable world of success.

My next memory, ironically, is of calling him up one day at his office at the *Jewish Frontier* to ask whether he and I could talk about some personal matter. Charles was most cordial in setting an appointment to visit me at my father's shop, which I had taken over during my father's illness. We were to have dinner in the neighborhood. The year was probably 1961, as I remember, in association with my father's illness and with my intention of selling the shop on his death. His death was near, and I was thinking of getting into work more congenial to me, such as editing or writing for a magazine. Once more, soft dreams of lower-middle-class success. And Charles at that time was, in effect, an editor on the *Jewish Frontier*.

I must have read his poems by that time since I had the temerity to call on him for help. How else could I have had the nerve to call him as one poet to another? After eventually overcoming my original reluctance, I *must* have taken my courage in hand and read him to discover, yes, we had something in common, but he was doing it differently. Well, I called him as one calls on a relative for help, and like a relative Charles responded. Had we been in touch before then? Why is my mind so reluctant to come forth with the facts of those years? (Am I seeking to forget, to overcome, to bathe in some kind of self-satisfying illusion about myself?) It was a desperate period for me, and I had only a few friends to call on for help and advice, and Charles was a long shot.

Of course, Charles was curious about my call. We sat across the table from each other at a neighborhood restaurant and talked about his job and my need for a job, perhaps one on the *Jewish Frontier* like his. Charles was gentlemanly, cordial, and responsive, and told me regretfully that his own job gave him a mere pittance toward survival and that there were no other opportunities at the office that he knew of. I believed him; I had no reason not to, seeing before me a man whose manner convinced me that he was in no better shape than I was. I began to like him deeply, and I began to appreciate our affinity. Everything he said to me at the table was directed toward my problem, with the gentlest expression of concern. I had met an elder brother with whom I could share my self and whose self was open to me, too. Charles insisted on paying for us both, though I had planned to take him to dinner, since it was I who had invited him. I see that gesture of his now as his way of sealing our new friendship.

Still, I was too far over my head in personal griefs and frustrations to harbor much thought about all that had taken place between us, yet, at his invitation, I went with him the following week to a printing shop where he oversaw the production of the *Jewish Frontier*. I watched as he carried out his duties with a kind of casual ease, a trait with which I had begun to identify him, though I could detect beneath this manner the sense of a man given over to his duties out of principle rather than out of pleasure in doing a good job. He would do a good job because his position of responsibility required it, and casual ease was a token of his approach: to be there on the spot, yet not with the body and feeling that he brought to things more deeply embedded in him. Otherwise, it would be a waste of the energy he hoarded for his more personal work. I felt how typical it was of a writer, recognizing it in myself. With this visit, we concluded one period of our friendship. I knew at that moment for a fact that I would have to make my way into the so-called literary world of publishing, or what have you, without his help. He was in need of help himself. He told me he was preparing yet another volume of his poems, also to be published at his own expense, and I felt even more that Charles had enough to do to keep himself afloat.

We were to meet again some years later at Brandeis University, to which Milton Hindus had invited us both to give readings. So it was apparent to others also that Charles and I had something in common as poets. Louis Zukofsky had been right, and though I had shied away from the thought, it was there all along in others, as it was in me. This time I would accept that connection. Charles and I had arrived at some recognition as poets, and we were to share it together. Of course, by this time, I was not only reading his poems but also studying them. Charles had given me several of his books and I, in turn, had given him my one and only. And yet I felt that his time for wider recognition had passed, and I was fearful that this would be the case for me, if only by association with him in the minds of others. I had not yet gotten over my worst sense of urgency—call it snobbishness—about American Success.

Time passed, my recognition was growing. I had published two more books, the second also paid for by me but the third accepted by Wesleyan University Press, and Charles too had begun to climb the success ladder, with a collected volume, *By the Waters of Manhattan,* New Directions, publisher. I was to give a reading at the Guggenheim Museum, and Charles was to introduce me. Simply, in the minds of many we were the younger and the older generation of working-class poets, both of whom reflected each other's interests in the city, with precise, concretely written poems, aphoristic and by turns painfully realistic. Charles did a fine job of introducing me, and I was pleased to have him there to do it.

Soon after, I began to teach in the New School for Social Research, having managed to escape the business world, the factory world. I was going to teach poetry as I understood and practiced it. So many students were writing in the abstract, mouthing platitudes about life and love—city students whose parents were in some kind of business, students who felt poetry had to rise above the sordid details of moneymaking to which their parents were bound, that it had to expostulate on the beauties that lay beyond working for a living, beyond the city life they lived in, with its grimy sidewalks, cockroaches, hurry, and tension. How was I to change their minds about the function of poetry, if not make poets of them? By changing their minds, I could at least let them see into the poetic process, appreciate its needs and its outcome. Who to begin with as a means? Charles Reznikoff, of course. *By the Waters of Manhattan,* naturally. I was absolutely delighted, relieved, and thankful to Charles at long distance. So things had come full circle. It was Charles and I who were the leading city poets in America, whether or not anyone else knew it as clearly as that. I knew it, and Charles knew it in his quiet persistence in publishing his own books, and we as working-class poets were slowly getting our due.

Other memories now come forward. I recall strolling with him along 5th Avenue one evening just before a reading at the Guggenheim by one of our poet friends. Charles was talking of his aborted career as a practicing lawyer, yet about having learned something in the process as a research assistant to successful lawyers, having learned of cases that fascinated him. That this experience had begun to shape in his mind his most ambitious undertaking, *Testimony,* I later could surmise from the intensity his voice took on, almost a singsong quality, in talking about it. But Charles only hinted at it. For he was his usual reticent self about his literary plans or work in progress, the complete opposite of me. After he spoke I complained loudly of the hardships attached to writing: the lack of time or energy after a day's work in business, much as I strove to plan or to push forward work in progress. And Charles, quickly changing tone, as if speaking for me, took up where I left off to tell me of his effort to write early in his life while employed in his parents' millinery factory. He was seeking to console me and by his own implied example, as editor, point to a brighter future for me. I was still operating the family bindery at the time, doing physically exhausting work. But the incident sticks in my mind after all these years. I had already begun taking Charles as a kind of mentor to me, almost unknowingly. It was not until later that night that I began to appreciate his relating to me his own experiences in factory life, recognizing this account as it was intended, as a help in getting through that difficult period. He was concerned.

And did he see in me a younger self who had succeeded in escaping factory days and who then looked forward to my escape? I wanted to believe it, and his kindness in hearing my complaints and answering as he did led me to believe he did care. Through the years, I felt Charles leading me to break with factory life. I would recall particular poems of his, with their profound compassion for people caught in the life of piece and hourly labor. I would find myself at work recalling whole poems of his. I could hear myself mouthing silently lines about city life. Our paths did not cross much in those days. After our meeting at the printing shop where he was overseeing the production of the *Frontier,* I launched on a determined campaign to escape, first by giving up my father's bindery at his death which had happened that same year after I had met Charles for dinner, then, as the plan went on, to ease my-self into some sort of managerial role in a larger bindery that would require less energy. The next step was to teach the writing of poetry during evenings at the New School for Social Research, as a foothold into the world to which I felt I rightfully belonged. It was all a demanding, closely monitored process and allowed no time for friendship as such, as I had conceived for Charles, though his poems echoed in my head.

And years were to pass before we were to meet again. Our next meeting is vivid to me. It was about a year or so before his death, when already his name was spoken everywhere, in colleges, librar-ies, institutions, and he was being called upon frequently to read in one place or another. He was in his late seventies, but constantly smiling, constantly in wonder at his growing fame, but never more modest. He had sent me the first volume of *Testimony,* and I was knocked over by it, by its calm account of cases of murder, lust, perversion, theft, and betrayals throughout the early years of this great republic. Each case was told with such economy of language, simplicity, and directness as to leave no doubt that we were read-ing an actual case drawn from legal history, but written from the viewpoint of an observer who could have been there. Fault was not the issue in these poems. It was more than that, it was the deepest sorrow and commiseration with pain, suffering, human frailty, with human limitation to self-understanding and self-disci-pline, with human lack of soul. He was revealing the grating isola-tion in which the victims and their aggressors lived in a country dedicated to unity within diversity. There was plenty of diversity but little or no unity, and the book was an overwhelming indictment of the case.

I knew Charles had written himself into a great poem with just this first installment. He was putting it all on the line. Finally, the bits and pieces, as I call them now, of his shorter poems, perfect as many are, had been gathered into his longest and most ambitious undertaking. Charles was speaking openly and loudly, once and for all, his most private thoughts: that he had not undertaken to practice law; that he had chosen instead to become an aid to his parents in their millinery business; that he had preferred to go from customer to customer selling them goods so that he could take notes on the existence of ordinary people in their ordinary rounds; that he preferred to be associated with them in person. All this was in growing awareness on his part of the true nature of American life he would not ignore or flee from into a comfortable middle-class existence. Yet he found solace in writing of observing the birds, trees, grass, and sky in his daily walks through the streets of the city, and occasionally he found solace in an individual in whom he found a kindred spirit or at least a spirit with which he could share his sense of the misery of the ordinary existence of this country's ordinary citizens. It was all in his poetry. Could a man do less than to write of his grief at the loss of opportunity this country once had? In his sardonic way Charles could only hope that something someday would cleanse this country of its shame. And so I was to find him on every page of *Testimony* speaking to me as he had not been able to in private on those occasions when we had met. After the first volume of *Testimony,* I felt closer to him than ever before.

Harvey Shapiro and I were to visit him at home one evening. Harvey, too, had been deeply struck by Charles's poems, perhaps sooner than I. To Harvey, Charles was the revelation of a truth he had been sensing through his own career as a teacher, editor, and free-lance writer, a different world from mine and from Charles's, yet a world from which Harvey suspected the truth was to be learned. Harvey having arranged this visit with Charles, I went along at his invitation.

I had sat in on one of Charles's readings and watched and listened. Young students almost everywhere were clamoring for his presence, an old man, nearly bald, stooped, modestly smiling, reading in an even conversational voice from poems filled with mayhem, cruelty, anger, but each poem presented calmly. The audience sat riveted, unable to stir or to sneeze to relieve themselves of the terror and compassion that ran through the poems.

The meeting between Harvey, Charles, and me went off with the greatest ease and cordiality. This, I realized a year or so later, was to be my last meeting with him. Charles was open and confiding of his feeling about himself and about others as I had not heard or observed before. We were poets to one another, identical spirits, and we drank our wine in that spirit. Charles was not satisfied, however, until he had given each of us at least three new books he had, again, printed at his own expense, and we left expecting to see him again one day, the gifts accepted in that belief and, because of that, with a certain air of casualness, at least on my part, believing I would have lots of time in which to read the books at leisure and comment on them to Charles when we again met. Hearing of his death months later—we had not corresponded nor talked by phone after the visit—I was baffled to have to believe what I was hearing, but I believe it now, in the sense that he had completed his most important work and was finished, as far as he was concerned, telling America what he thought of it, and waited in his grave patiently for American to digest it.

15. Charles Olson

It was very brief. Charles Olson called me long distance from North Carolina, as I was supervising a shopful of working people in my father's pamphlet bindery sometime during the fifties. I stood in the midst of huge folding machines slamming away at their jobs, my ears roaring, and could barely hear him tell me in a high-pitched voice that he wanted me to come out to Black Mountain College to live and teach. I'd have a house and a garden—no salary, but I'd be taken care of. In other words, I wouldn't starve, and I'd be among fellow poets and very happy in a most congenial atmosphere. I agreed with him absolutely on this last point and I laughed. I had to laugh. At that moment, his proposition was so absurd for me and so tragically late. If he had gotten in touch with me a year earlier, I'd have jumped at his invitation. I wouldn't have committed myself to helping my aging father run his shop.

As he talked, trying to persuade me, I kept repeating between his rapid sentences that I would give it thought, that I very much doubted it, and that I would talk it over with my wife, and I would think of how I could disentangle myself from my commitment to my father. It seemed unlikely as I talked. I didn't know who I could turn to to take my place. Olson hung up disappointed, and I raced back to the workers who were standing idly waiting for me to give them their orders for the day.

But the incident has lingered with me, its significance growing with the years. By my refusal to join him, I had defined myself as unalterably of the striving middle class, with its goals and ambitions and ideals. Nor could I conceive how I could benefit from the stay at Black Mountain College. I had published my first volume, which Williams had praised lavishly in a review in *The New*

York Times Book Review. It was this review probably and, I hoped, a reading of my book that convinced Olson to call me, but I already was convinced in my own mind that I did not need any further guidance or company in my ambition to write than I got in my association with Williams. He was the real thing. The others were his students in one way or another. Besides, I had this very practical bent pounded into me by my circumstances, my upbringing, my marriage, my child—the thought that money in this country played a vital role in one's well-being and that without it I might not become the poet I aspired to become.

It was a paradox, for sure, in romantic ethics, but I did not see myself as a romantic poet. I saw myself as a tragic poet, not as a poet of the land, a pastoral poet, as Black Mountain College seemed to suggest for me. I was a poet of the city, where the action was inside and outside, and despite the excruciating trials I had to endure as a business person, with the hope all the while of emerging from it—just a wisp of a hope—I felt that here was my place in the scheme of things. Williams thought so too, and that more than helped me to stick with it. It settled me permanently into the role of a poet of the city.

All this was at the back of my mind when I had regretfully to refuse Olson's invitation, which I had brought home to my wife, who looked at me in expectation. She was used to the unexpected from me, and a sudden reversal of my direction would not come as a surprise to her. I told her sorrowfully that I was turning down the invitation. I had for a long while wanted to live in the countryside in the illusion that it would be a more leisurely life, which for some obscure reason I associated with the countryside. I did want to get away from the pressures of city life long enough to feel myself rested. I did want to ease my life somewhat and perhaps, perhaps, change my life altogether. My wife, sympathetic with my circumstances, nevertheless understood my reluctance to accept Olson's invitation and went along with my decision to decline. But Williams's praise was one thing; having to live the life he envisioned for me was something else. Although I did have a kind of reservation at assuming the role of the city poet, knowing from firsthand experience its grueling effects on me, by finally settling down to it, I knew I was refusing Olson because the pattern of my life had been set for me early in my life, partly through my love of Whitman's poems about the city, life in the great metropolis, and partly because I felt that my withdrawal from the urban experience would be a confession of weakness and fear, an act of regression, especially in a world becoming steadily urban. The life of the people of the world was being shaped by urban life, and I felt I had to be in at the center.

16. Louis Zukofsky

My outstanding memory of Louis Zukofsky is of being seated with him at his house on Willow Street in Brooklyn during the fifties, when Pound was yet hospitalized at St. Elizabeths. Louis had no apologies for the correspondence that had gone on between them before, during, and after the war, though he recognized the enigmatic nature of their relationship. Louis's emphasis druing our conversation about Pound was on the aesthetic theory and practice he felt he had in common with him. It was not as if he was placing these above Pound's political, social, and racial views and prejudices. It was as if this aesthetic remnant of the man had to be preserved. That Louis had a personal stake in preserving this faded glory of Pound's I recognized from the beginning. I was then only awakening to Louis's poetic debt to his mentor and his most important teacher. Still, I was not about to condemn Louis for his defense. I respected Louis too much as a poet, while my own feelings toward Pound were ambivalent, at best. I not only respected Pound as poet but had learned from him too, and so when the topic turned to his racial views and prejudices I would find myself suspending judgment, if only for Louis's sake, Louis who was so deeply attached to Pound as man too. It had come through to me in my conversation with Louis that Pound had been more than kind to him, in fact, had treated him in letters as a brother.

For me, it was a perplexing situation. Louis was an older man than I, and in a way a mentor to me. I looked to him, among other important figures, such as Williams, for approval of my poems, and so I would listen closely when Louis discussed Pound, and I remember how often I would bring our conversation around to the subject, out of continued puzzlement and sometimes anxiety, when

I would suddenly begin to doubt Louis's judgment of the man, for there was a menacing quality to Pound, the fear of which I could not entirely suppress in Louis's company. He had gone to visit Pound at St. Elizabeths and had returned home saddened. Their meeting at the hospital had been friendly enough, but Pound's mental state grieved Louis. He felt and said candidly that the man had boxed himself in with his political, social, and racial views and now was paying a steep price in emotional anguish and disorientation. It was not the Pound with whom he had corresponded for years. Louis, saddened, concerned, touched me deeply. Knowing as he did, as he openly commented on to me, of Pound's virulent attacks against the Jews, of whom Louis was one quintessentially, yet his own compassion seemed boundless. It was the man who touched Louis, the deterioration mentally and emotionally of a once great, seminal figure. I did not bring up the subject again, consciously, in the year that followed. I knew I had reached the pith of Louis's anguish. It was enough for me to know that in his way Louis shared my own wracked ambivalence.

My view of Louis as poet has been ambivalent too, but in a wholly different way. I could enjoy and value with a continual attachment his poems of love to Celia and Paul, his wife and son. Knowing his family, I could see where these poems came from but even more important I could recognize their artistic discipline in getting the theme and tone on paper. He was a marvelously fine artist in projecting this most intimate part of himself, his attachment to and love of his immediate family. It was what I envied in him as a poet. I myself had yet to find my conscious style and my subject in full awareness of it, as he long ago had discovered for himself, and so his beautiful domestic poetry was a guidepost on my journey toward self-realization.

It was with his extraordinarily, for him, long poem, *A,* that I had and still have the only important difficulty. Its intellectuality, giving preference to knowledge and judgments of knowledge of others and events in an aura of schematic thinking has made me resistant to the poem, particularly as I would recall his lovely short poems of love and wit. Should I say now that it is incumbent upon me that I begin to reread this poem, that I have left it in abeyance in my mind, as well as in fact, for these many years? To tell the painful truth, I had a fear of meeting with him socially precisely because of my inability to appreciate this poem, and so we were to meet only on rare occasions during the sixties when the poem began to emerge in its fullness, and then at my own self-invitation after working up my courage. I would avoid talk about it, but I would offer him and Celia my honest affection, my deep respect for his dedication to his art and his intransigence toward convention and tradition in poetry and toward those who practiced them. I was not honest in avoiding discussion of *A* when it probably would have delighted Louis to clarify its problem for me. On the one or two occasions when I timidly and obliquely asked for enlightenment I did not gain clearer understanding nor greater appreciation either, and so I let further opportunities slip by and we talked instead about mutual family matters. If Louis recognized my reluctance, he gave no hint of it in his jovial moods, but I was filled with guilt toward him, though he was always kind. At the publication of each of my volumes I would send him a copy and would receive back promptly a brief but succinct characterization of the book, always complimentary. His spirit is with me still and I can yet hear that nasal voice, sometimes cranky, sometimes complaining, but more often witty and affectionate and cheerful toward his friends. I can hear him in his shorter poems, and I will search for him in his masterpiece.

🞥 17. Stanley Kunitz 🞥

I do not read Stanley Kunitz's poems as a critic would, from a detached, aesthetic position. My long identification with him through his poems has made that impossible or, better yet, eliminated its relevance for me. This identification began many years ago at the start of my writing career. We are a generation apart in the literary influences upon our work, but I was from the beginning of my career fascinated how one man could contain such pressing and powerful emotions within traditional forms invented with the purpose of supporting and illustrating in themselves an elegant accommodation to life. Many of Kunitz's poems for me nearly wrenched themselves free of these forms with images and phrases that seemed to jar the poems out of their smooth paths, but craftsman that he is he retained control. The spirit of play that activated the forms was carried through with a master's hand. Reading him during those apprenticeship days, I would discuss with myself how it was possible to keep one's sense of self intact while releasing emotions of such overwhelming force onto the page. It was precisely in the play of traditional controls that Kunitz was able to vent his emotions of anger, fear, guilt, and despair.

What a marvelous balance of forces exists in many of his poems between utter and extreme feeling and the saving art with which they are written. The poem, becoming an embodiment of feeling, becomes also a triumph over feeling, even if momentarily. I well remember coming upon "The Science of the Night" for the first time and thinking, "Here is a poet whose example I can follow: how to turn private tragedy into an art that communicates itself to the reader and, through the reader's understanding of and identification with the poem, becomes an emotional support by his pleasure in the art." In "The Science of the Night," rising from the matrix of pain out of which the poem is formed, is exactly that joyousness in language, that love of communication as art by which I could identify with the poem and through it with the poet. I saw Kunitz in this poem rescuing himself from drowning in grief, an act that he had initiated of his own will to affirm his life, for his art is an affirmation of his life.

What further added to my conviction that we had much in common were the issues of and questions about life basic to his poems. A mere ten years in age separated us, but we were each in our own way experiencing the traumatic thirties and forties, Kunitz as an alienated and isolated poet and scholar in a world desperately at loss with itself, a world slowly but inexorably drifting toward dissolution of its will and soon to be plunged into war. Between the private and public man there could be no saving division in a maelstrom that sucked everything into itself and spewed forth wreckage. Wreckage was what Kunitz was writing about with enormous bravura, and wreckage was what I was writing about grimly. Alone with myself, I looked for confirmation of my vision in the writings of others as I wrote my poems, and those by Kunitz came to light for me in the libraries I frequented in search of intellectual and emotional companionship. I had only to read him to realize I had met my contemporary. How much of my own life I read into his poems I need not go into here, but the more I absorbed of the work of this newly discovered poet—his magnificently angry political and social poems, his poignant family losses—the deeper grew my conviction that I was not alone.

It was with the publication of *The Testing Tree,* which decisively broke with his past style, that I realized Kunitz was signaling a profound change in himself. As I soon came to realize, I had seen this change coming earlier in his translations from the Russian, but I did not then grasp its meaning for Kunitz. The translations were adaptations into fine-honed free form from strict Russian forms. That he chose to translate fixed verse patterns into equally beautiful versions in an opposite style came as a surprise to me and a welcome one, if only because it indicated to me Kunitz's ability to cope with change, but it was not until the publication of *The Testing Tree* that I recognized the full implications for Kunitz as poet and man.

Of course, I may only conjecture about what actually took place within the man, and it is as conjecture that I write this, relying on evidence that I believe is there in his poems for others to see. Those emotions that in his earlier closed forms were about to spill over were present still at high heat in poems of *The Testing Tree*, particularly in the title poem itself, but there was a significant difference. In this new book he had created a distinctly felt distance from these emotions. It was as if he had arrived at some accommodation, not with closed forms, as in the past, but with himself. He seemed willing to view and even to express these same doubts, anger, guilts, and despairs with a sense that could have come only from an inner peace. Serenity is the word for it in common speech.

How Kunitz arrived at this state of mind is for him to tell. Nevertheless, it is there in even the more recent poems in his latest book, *The Poems of Stanley Kunitz, 1928–78*. The juxtaposition of past and present styles in this latest book, however, inevitably raises the question, an important question in view of an extraordinary change, as to its cause or causes. One theory might be that the new and relaxed inner condition has been able to work this transformation in his art too. Another theory might be that the aesthetics of the open form may have had its attraction for Kunitz and been equally the cause of his change from traditional verse forms. Still another opinion might hold that the aesthetics of the open form and the change from within coincided and acted upon one another to bring forth the change in both spheres, the man and the artist. However the change of style did come about, it has, in its way unique to the practice of the open form, lent a tone and address that were not, at least in those early days, available to him.

A romantic myth persists among certain critics and poets that by abandoning the revered classical forms we also abandon inten-

sity of language and vision, replacing it with prose and the ano-
nymity of language that, as is claimed, is characteristic of prose.
The truth is exactly the opposite. For those who have worked
steadily and long in the so-called open free form (I wish it were
possible to name it more accurately; it is a name given not to indi-
cate release from form but from form imposed from without)
know how difficult an art it is to write from an inner vision that
tolerates no other form but that which it perceives in itself. Such a
vision cares neither for what has come before it in manner, nor for
what will come after it, but only for its own unique existence. It
strives for its authentic self, independent of others. There is no
venture in the arts more exacting, challenging, and risky, and more
significant. It is the product of profound confidence in one's own
inner resources not only to write the poem of such exacting de-
mand but to have the desire to do so, out of absolute conviction of
its rightness and importance for the poet and the person. In *The
Testing Tree* and in his more recent poems, Stanley Kunitz suc-
ceeds with honor.

It certainly could not have come easily. It had to be the testing
of himself too in the change of style he was undertaking. What I
read in his latest poems is that he has freed himself of enormous
internal pressures by a deepened insight into them. And so he has
found the form or forms to correspond to this freedom and open-
ness. It is in change precisely that we discover the character
and meaning of Kunitz and his poems, change that expresses itself
in outrage at social and political injustice, change that struggles
with private guilts and despairs. Is this not the character out of
which freedom is born? If Kunitz in his poems is a figure of
change, is it not also appropriate to state that he also is the poet
in search of his freedom from oppression internal and external?
Now that he has declared himself openly by a change of his forms
of verse to the forms that are the very signs of his freedom, is this
not a character fulfilled, of the highest order? To miss the man
for the aesthetic complexities that attend change is to be less the

critic than the pedant. In Kunitz we have a resource in these days by which to help ourselves toward that freedom that each person craves.

In an introduction I gave to a reading by Kunitz, I sum up for myself the significance of this man, his life and work, as I have gathered it from my years of study and living with his words and of seeing the man himself in his relationships. It reads as follows: "Societies ideally are formed of communion with and compassion for others. If our society had to choose one poet to express in his person and in his art those difficult ideals about itself, it would choose Stanley Kunitz, for aesthetics are not the issue in his poems; they are made of the deepest concerns with ways to live, and in his search as one man among us he has made poetry of it, the poetry of our deepest needs. There is no higher art. He has brought life to art, and in his art our difficult lives are passionately affirmed."

18. James Wright

About Jim, I feel as I do about life: He's there; he's available; he's open. He gives you what he has, and to look for something beneath or above or within is not to understand life or Jim. He is all there is, and he is telling us that we all live it all at once inside, outside, above and below, simultaneously. Take any one of his poems. Read it for what it says, for its sound, for its subject, and if you don't grasp that this man is giving you the facts of what it is to live . . .

He's the kind of man who can't lie. He's absolutely helpless when it comes to lying, and so he has to tell the truth in a crunch, that is, when he's writing the poem; when the poem must be written; when there's no way out of it except through it; no avoiding it, forgetting it or delaying it, as when a person sits in the witness box and the prosecutor is there, hammering away at the person. What else can you do but tell the truth? A lie would come stumbling out under such pressure, and so the person tells the truth and feels relieved, even if he has convicted himself. But Jim doesn't care about that. Being convicted is old stuff to him. Every poem he writes convicts him, and he keeps living and going back to the desk to write again, to place himself in the open, the way life is always out in the open.

What choice does he have? None. He is what life is, even if for the moment he thinks that he is different, that he is an intellect, an objective being who can make decisions, order himself to do this or that or order anything, like a master or a god. He knows then that he'd be lying, and so he goes back to the desk after a very heated exchange between him and the prosecutor in which he had to admit openly his implication in that last case. There's another on his desk, and he's going to go through with it again.

Pleasure? For the sake of pleasure in it? Don't kid yourself. Is there pleasure in opening a closet with a dead body in it? There's a duty to open the closet. Jim opens it, and he does find a pleasure in having committed himself to opening the door. You guessed it: Inside the closet that body had begun to stir at the approach of his steps, and as he opens the door grimly, in expectation of a dead body, out steps a lively, talking, exultant man, and they embrace. This is the pleasure: two brothers who have found each other. Jim does this day after day, opening closets, finding brothers and sisters too. He is not afraid.*

As each of you may have experienced at some time in your life, the voice of a major poet is instantly recognized. One doesn't say too much about it to those who know, since they have their own sense of it. I will say briefly what I could say inexhaustibly for my own pleasure and awe, that James Wright is a chanter of the nation, an Homeric voice embracing the self, standing, falling, rising, or staggering to his life. He made it the metaphor of our land, for who else could write of the ultimate defeat each of us experiences as if it were the flight of birds back to the earthy wilderness for survival? In James Wright's poetry, we who have taken refuge in ourselves have found a yea sayer who has discovered the way, through a bitter spiritual odyssey of his own. He was born and raised at this country's navel of blast furnaces and sprawling shack towns in the Midwest, from where issue the advertised good things of our life and our tragic world position. The drunks, the addicted, the dissolute in body and mind, the despairing successful, the absolute failures, and the voluntary castoffs of our system—all are in this poetry, together with that beauty that

* This piece was written in 1978. James Wright died on March 25, 1980, after a prolonged illness.

is its own affirmation, that is of the whole being, be it wrecked
or dying.

Listen to the language, written in praise and in pity, robust yet
tender, committed to love and imaginative release. The renascence
in American literature that began in the Midwest in the very be-
ginning of the twentieth century and produced the universally ac-
claimed Sherwood Anderson and Theodore Dreiser can add to its
enduring record the truth, the wild, Surrealist tenderness of James
Wright's poetry.

❦ 19. Paul Zweig ❧

My last meeting with Paul Zweig took place in 1984 about three months before his annual summer departure for Dordogne, France, where he owned a house and small farm. Paul then was desperately ill but hopeful of yet another ten years of life, as told him by his doctors, and so he was to leave feeling that at least within these ten years he could accomplish the main body of his planned work, such as the Walt Whitman book and his third book of poems. We parted on an intimate, hopeful note about his future, because his doctors had also revealed to him that a remission was not to be ruled out altogether, since by the use of chemotherapy he was holding his own against the dread lymphatic cancer. He looked well and sturdy, he talked animately as always, with sharp asides of his opinions on the writings of other poets and prose writers whom he did not entirely respect, yet with an exalted tone of admiration for those in whom he felt great talent and accomplishments. He was in every sense of the word a deeply generous and sympathetic man, with the highest literary standards to guide him in his judgments. His book on Whitman is shaped by his profound love and empathetic identification with Whitman.

After his death in Paris in the summer of 1984, I was to learn from others close to him that during the three months between my meeting with him and his departure for Dordogne he was given an estimate of his life span grimly revised to perhaps three more years. Nevertheless, he flew to France with his wife and daughter. His sudden death, a shock to all of us, was not unexpected, as it was not by Paul. His last words were to his wife, Vikki, "I love you," and to his closest friend, the poet C. K. Williams, "Good-bye, my friend." He died, exalted in his loves, as in life.

Walt Whitman: The Making of the Poet is also about the spiritual growth of Paul in his last years, as he himself was to realize. Its passionate search for the truth was in Paul's character; its brilliant, incisive prose style was of Paul's temperament; his deep sympathy for Whitman's emotional life was for all of us; and his artistry in bringing together seemingly disparate and fragmentary materials was in Paul's need to make of life a wholly understandable phenomenon for our sake and his as well. The essential man and poet is in the book, and we are thankful for having shared his life with him.

~ 20. Simon Perchik ~

Whoever first reads Simon Perchik's poems thinks the writer is having a bad dream; no two words seem to fit together, as we expect in everyday speech and as we expect in contemporary poetry, which long ago took on the characteristics of everyday speech. But Simon, precisely because he considered himself as part of that contemporary tradition, for years without realizing his special difference, wrote straight from inner perception, a method, too, that he had deduced from reading the poetry of his contemporaries. So he felt free, along with others, to write from within and to write in a style that concentrated on the image, another contemporary tradition that he believed he was honoring in adhering strictly to it in his poems. And so, the new reader of his work may ask what then makes Simon Perchik's work so different from that of his fellow poets. He is an original.

Simon's art is that of the painter on canvas, and in the Surrealist mode, at that, when he is most extreme in his style. To understand him, literally to be able to read him clearly as we read the work of most of his contemporaries, we cannot depend upon the order of his words, nor on his syntax, nor on the idiom—on none of the details that go to form the modern American style. Simon takes all of them into his hands and, as it would seem, throws them high into the air to watch them land upon the page. But it is not without thought or plan. We will choose the phrase, the image, the punctuation that suits his theme best, as they land on the page from high up. His intention is to present a picture of what he is thinking, rather than a statement, a picture that implicitly leads one to his thought and feeling. To Simon, thought and feeling are merged and represented by the picture, the image, and if his thought is complex and sometimes involuted, with huge jumps of perception, then the images, the pictures must faithfully do the same. You, the reader, must be able to see, as on a canvas, the connection, say, between a watermelon and a tenement house, as they appear on the canvas side by side or one on top of the other or one inside the other. There is no other hint or suggestion on what is meant. That is for you to work out as imagery, imagery traditionally associated with meaning. In fact, there is no image Perchik uses that is not familiar to the modern reader in everyday life, but woe to the reader who thinks the image of a radiator is meant simply to convey the association with heat, with winter. No, it could mean that Simon recognizes the possibility of a radiator being viewed as a saddle for a horse, and he will let you know through the full colon which comes after the image of a rider, followed by the image of a radiator.

One may think all this some kind of illegitimate poetry, not poetry at all but simple incompetence to say what he wants to say, an inability to speak plainly, to make himself understood, as American poetry today prides itself on doing, but Simon is himself, as American poetry quixotically demands. He is authentically himself, as American poetry prescribes. Then what is wrong? For one, he lacks the expected music or cadence of the line. He emphasizes connections or disconnections between images, and these usually come in short bursts of perception, giving way to still another and yet another.

When you look at a Surrealist painting, you do not look for the rhythms in which the images should, according to conventional taste, be present in a painting, that is, a conventional, purely realistic painting by, say, Jack Levine, the archking of realist painters. In Dali or in Ernst, we are met by powerful oddities staring us in the face, challenging us to make sense of them or sense of ourselves as we absorb the work, or find ourselves unable to or refuse. Simon Perchik himself will protest, and has protested to me in the past, that he does not consider himself a Surrealist poet. He is certain that with a little straining of the imagination by the reader, with a free flow of association by the reader, all will become clear. Well, it does not always happen that way. Our tradition has dried up that particular flow. We are used to being fed, spoon fed, virtually, by the simplicity of language, by its faithful reproduction of idiom, diction, sound, pace, as they make themselves felt in American poetry. That being the case, we have no choice at this stage in our development as poets and readers but to call Perchik at least a quasi-Surrealist. It is our problem. We need to be more closely attentive, we need to begin to exercise our atrophying internal life. Simon Perchik, as poet, is here to stay, and as one in a community of poets, should be welcomed into the fold. He can teach us how to be different from each other, as we think we are, but need to be reminded by one like Perchik that the difference should be original, not a stale variant on an old, worn practice.

What can be said of Perchik's education and upbringing that could convey more of an understanding and appreciation of his accomplishment? I don't believe that such an obvious connection exists, which again, to me, is in the spirit of his quasi-disjunctive style. If anything, his life as a lawyer, family man, methodical being, sociable and affectionate to his friends, certainly belies his inner world. Perchik, retired from law, having for several years served as a prosecuting attorney for Suffolk County in the field of pollution, leads a most regulated life of writing and study and the occasional social affairs he allows himself to participate in. In short, he is a dedicated writer and an affectionate father and husband and friend. Make of this, if you can, the character of a writer of disjunctive poetry, often verging on the inexplicable, the Surrealist mode.

21. Not One Voice but Many

In 1971 I wrote an essay, "The Necessity of the Personal," which was subsequently published in my book *Open Between Us*. In it, as the title indicates, I make a case for the personal voice in American poetry as the only true authentic mode, given our social and cultural tradition of the individual at the center of his society and culture. I have since found nothing to contradict this statement, even in poetry as seemingly exotic and arcane as that of John Ashbery, or, for that matter, in the poetry of Charles Bernstein and his colleagues in their pursuit and development of "Language Poetry." For me, the style of each poet—Ashbery, Bernstein, and followers—is always one I can identify with the poet, and I would not find it interesting or of significance if, by chance or design or loss of confidence, the poet adopted a style foreign to him.

In that essay, I stress over and over that the strength and genius of American poetry as currently written is in the multitudinous voices we hear coming from every part of the country. It is, ultimately, the epic we are searching for in American poetry, the combined sounds in a national chorus. There is no other way it can be defined for me. Otherwise, as single poets we are writing of a small patch of territory, ourselves and our immediate environment and uniqueness of voice, but when we have said that, we have said everything there is to say about the poet. There is almost nothing to say beyond that. An Ashbery or a Robert Bly or a June Jordan speaks for himself or herself, but when we place them side by side, along with the myriad good poets writing today, we have magnificence. We have Whitman's America, tragic as it is in its delusions of empire and world domination. Each poet contributes his or her understanding of the underlying ill in American life, and the total is more rounded, deeper, and more worthy of study than any statistical studies and psychological studies.

And so there is an American poetry now, but written not by any one source exclusively. We have poets of the South, Charles Wright and Wendell Berry, in the Southwest, Ai. We have William Stafford, Michael McClure, and Diane Wakoski, of the Far West; and so forth, East and North. They can be named by the score in each part of the country. If anyone were to try to define American poetry as exclusively Far West, he or she would be violating the very principle that makes for so much exuberance, authenticity, and abundance, precisely what Whitman had hoped for. But of course, it is only since the 1950s that Whitman has been accepted for his national stature, and yet the academicians are once more in the process of reversing this role by forming small but effective circles of admiration around specific poets to the exclusion of others, with the purpose of raising one poet above all the others, in total disregard of the basic drive in American culture for a democratic alliance among all of us. The academicians must have hierarchies; the poets must have community. The conflict, if it continues its present trend, will destroy American poetry at its roots. The authentic American poetry is not one voice but many.

III. The One with the Many

⚛ 22. A Poet ⚛
Is Not Autonomous

I realize that your questions are stunning, if not impossible to answer as categorically as they are stated. For a poet to tell you* what he is doing in poetry, where he expects to go in poetry, and what he thinks others are doing, not to speak of his differences with them and with past poets—man, you're asking for a book of poems! That is what poetry is about, all this that you throw at us in the form of questions. We have to work these thoughts out slowly through the writing of poems, not through essays. Get what I mean? Wouldn't it be just as simple and perhaps equally interesting for you and your colleagues to read the poets of whom you have requested essays to seek to make your own conjectures about each poet's future, differences, and qualities? You probably would come up with the right answers, on the whole.

Honestly, I can't tell you where I'm going as poet or what devices I'm about to use or intend to use. This would be idiotic for a poet to reply to, plainly. How do I know that tomorrow I might not burst out of my regular bonds to become another kind of person, maybe fall in love with a meteor or whatever that suddenly pulls at my insides like a huge magnet, sets free all the inhibitions I have practiced for years, and sends me zooming in poetry and life into an outer space of no social structure, where I float like a seed in spring: disaster: I float down in mud or swamp. I don't know which. What kind of devices will I use to free myself of my

* This piece was originally written in response to questions implied in the sentence "For a poet to tell you. . . ."

condition? Don't you see that your question is irrelevant to the writing of poetry- The *actual* writing of poetry.

William Carlos Williams said more than once that the writing of poetry is 99 percent living. I find that technique, and differences from other poets in what I have to say and what I have not to say, are not under my control every day of the week, damn it. That's what all this bitching is about in the world. We don't know where we're going, and we don't know what we're doing, and we don't know what to expect next. Who expected the sordid mess of Vietnam in this country? You? Johnson? Who? Nobody, absolutely nobody, and now go find the techniques and differences, and so on, that will define it, make sense of it, and relieve us of it.

Now do you see how naive are the questions you ask? We struggle like flies upon water, like flies on flypaper. We are not autonomous beings and will never be. We don't want to be autonomous, we want to be told, to be cradled and assured and directed in the kindly spirit that keeps assuring us we have lovely souls and mean good, even if we do evil. Orthodox Puritanism is dead, but you formulate your questions out of the sanguine belief that we are each in possession of our soul, or have a soul to save. Ridiculous. Poetry is written in an attempt to rescue this so-called soul, this sense of independence, from complete collapse, and whatever techniques you seek or use are dependent on the nature of the beast you must confront at that time. But how often can you save your sense of independence from collapse without finally collapsing on yourself? In other words, writing poetry is a futile attempt at saving oneself from annihilation. It happens, despite our best efforts, and when we have reached that stage of realization then we begin to write out of resignation. Oddly enough, the poetry then becomes even finer than before. Note Eliot and Williams, Yeats and Dylan Thomas at the very ends of their lives. I've reached the end of this and keep moving into the blinking dark, leaving you behind to follow later, later.

❧ 23. The Self and the Other ❧

Here I am saying that Stevens misses the essential point in "Esthetique du Mal" when he separates the principle of imagination from the principle of reality. Both are characterized by change and the possibility of seeing one thing in terms of another. So that imagination and so-called reality or chaos, as he would have it, had he gone further, would have turned out to be the same thing. The thought then presents itself as to the function of reality in existing—purpose, better said. The purpose, then, is as the purpose of imagination, to maintain a lively attitude toward matter, to see in matter its own metamorphosis from being to being. Since all is matter, we are all in the same cauldron of change, together with the stars and the grass. We are in reality and never out of it. We are reality. We do not form imaginative wholes or fictions with which to defend ourselves against reality. We are doing precisely the same thing as is the chaotic reality, changing, ever changing its face, simply carrying out the principle of being or reality in its constant movement toward and from itself, the very character and nature of reality as we manifest it in our imaginative existence in poetry and all the human arts and events.

Chaos is us, if we must have it that way, according to Stevens, but since we live and breathe and function beyond and with and by and against and toward and away from pain, we cannot honestly declare all this chaos, ourselves chaos who live to know, to see, to change, which too is within the principle of being. We are immune from destruction ultimately on the transcendent level, though change is us in changing into age and another aspect of ourselves in death. I have here the whole of my philosophy, with Stevens's help.

Addendum

It is inane to say that because we imagine reality in our image that this too is a fiction. The fiction is that we pretend to create fictions that separate us from reality, since we are the reality. We are projecting a schizoid behavior and that too is a reflection of reality. No matter what we do we cannot tear ourselves apart. We cannot wrest ourselves from the universe. We are together with the air, the stars, the principle of gravity.

The division between ego and reality is a false one because the ego manifests exactly the principle that makes reality reality, and that is change, renewal, reassertion, reaffirmation of itself in constant emerging new forms: an expression of its ability/capacity as reality as ego seeks constant satisfaction in affirmation of itself in new triumphs of imposition or domination or conversion.

Have I arrived at my fulfillment as a writer and poet, which explains my sense of being in balance with myself? This is the aesthetic explanation, and yet I'm not prepared to plunge into active politics or any extraliterary activities, as I prefer waiting for that inspirational moment, the aesthetic that will get me writing again out of pleasure with the image.

This could be bad news. I've never or rarely written for the pleasure in the image. Typically, I need an emotive force to start me writing and it's this emotive force that produces the imagery; so it's true to say that now I feel no emotive force in me or upon me from other sources. I am in a kind of stasis. Call me a tree and be done with it, or worse, a stick of wood content to lie in the rain and be kicked around by kids, without complaint, finding pleasure in simply being a stick of wood, and suddenly I see an old workingman in overalls, as it were, the metaphor for what I'm saying— the worker who is content with his work and his wages, perhaps, in any case, content with his skills and his status in the trade, while high above him are several operators in their booths manipulating his work and his skills.

Some kind of spiritual deepening/awakening is needed to resolve my contradictions. If I believe men and women need to be good to one another, then I must fulfill all the obligations of such a tenet. I should subordinate my writing to my duties to others. Perhaps because it goes the other way with me I feel empty all the time, self-conscious about writing the poem. I can't stand writing the poem for its own sake, simply to demonstrate to myself my ability to turn out a well-made arrangement of words: art for art's sake. I'm not that breed and yet I envy their self-enclosed, self-delighting ways. I guess I'm divided in myself, first because writing, even when it is hotly emerging from an emotive force, must, to be effective, have a character, a style of its own, and that means for the poet an attention to language, a pleasure in finding the right words. Still, I'm assured in myself that such a pleasure is at the service of a much larger issue, the poem for the reader, the poem of communication, with the reader participating in the poet's emotions and values through the medium of the poet's language, rather than as in "fine art," enjoying the language for its own sake.

Art for art's sake has its roots in a philosophy or attitude that says that each man or woman lives strictly for himself or herself and creates out of his or her own need, without regard for other issues. It's as if the individual were sheltered, removed from society in some sort of protective cocoon in the midst of turmoil and war and could produce like a flower and for the sake of the flower. Underlying this attitude is still another and very despairing one, that each person is born alone to live alone and to be self-delighting until the end. There is truth in this, but each is born individually, a difference from being born alone, and each person lives individually and is self-delighting to demonstrate, to affirm individuality.

A thought occurs to me that individuality is equated with aloneness and that this is the root of the attitude. If individuals feel themselves alone, it is because they have no pleasure in their individuality, see no connection with others, do not grasp that the individual is an organic component of society, see no society around them, do not feel it within themselves. What is to be done? If such is the situation for a certain individual, then the problem is grave: how to infuse such a person with his or her own social worth and significance. But many are interested in extending themselves to help such a person and how many in such an isolated existence can or care to reach out for the hand that is willing to touch theirs?

We're at an impasse here and the answer is to simply go on as before, tolerating art for art's sake as a kind of aberration in the sense of a profound error.

The tension in a room with married couples is the undercurrent of rebelliousness toward conventional behavior, especially as the people get to know each other better and in a more relaxed atmosphere. The tension is reduced but the inhibitions become more obvious among them. Eros in prison.

I'm a wise old man of literature among poets, but I refuse to create about myself a studied manner. I'm a wise old man dancing on his creaky shanks, amazing the young with my antics. I refuse to take my age seriously and they refuse to believe that I am as bouncy as I make out to be, but I am spirited because I have experienced old age and youth and now have nothing else to fear, not even death. I already have lived through it by passing from one stage of my life to the present, and I shall be a hardy worm springing from my flesh, all its brothers underground. Nothing can kill me. I am always alive.

As writer and poet, I really don't know who I represent besides myself, and so I often feel futile and ridiculous as a writer with pretensions to national, even international importance. I feel silly, to say the least, and wish to go hide myself and my talent for shame, I am so little in my own eyes.

How does one know who one writes for? When I hear of this and that person gasping with pleasure at my work or at seeing me in the flesh, I wonder who is sane in this instance. How can I delight myself over such effusive attention and praise when I feel so unsure of myself, particularly since I do not know the person or his or her qualifications as a reader cultivated in the art of poetry? Knowing nothing about this person, except his or her brightened expression in language or in features, I am embarrassed for myself. It seems to me at the moment that it is ignorance or naivete or desire to gain something from me that would cause such an emotional upheaval in a person. Surely, I argue with myself, a person knowledgeable in the poetic art would take it all for granted in me, if such were the judgment of that person, and greet me as a peer on my own level of social calm and casualness, and that's all!

But then sometimes I am inclined to think, from the evidence before me in speech and manners and bearing, that overly enthusiastic persons are from a background like mine. I am especially struck by that thought, and when they begin that effusive routine, I flinch, but then I slowly relax before them and accept them casually—indifferently is more like it. I feel I've gained my freedom from them long, long ago, my stature with them assured for always. I become impatient with them, they become uneasy before me. They sense a current of hostility in me. Where were they when I first started out? Would they have been as enthusiastic in support of me then as they are now in my present "elevated" position? Who knows? I suppose I would find among them others like myself struggling to free themselves.

The city diminishes me. I had the experience recently of two days spent partly in walking the street, eating in restaurants, and living in a shabby, unpainted apartment, in each instance invaded by noises of traffic, sirens, voices. Crowds were going in all directions like disorderly civilian armies. I had only to enter their ranks to become one of them, and as I did that for several hours on the street, I began to feel myself not as David Ignatow, the poet and professor, but the man walking on the left of the lady in a brown coat behind a man in a blue suit, on the right of a blind woman led by a dog. But the arrangement and figures kept changing, and

I had no way of getting to know these others in the army with me, as they had no chance to know and talk to me. We either slipped into doorways or turned corners or dived down into subways or ran across the street to hail a cab.

How could I count myself important and outstanding in such a situation? I gave up. I went with the crowd. I grew numb and mechanical about my goal, and when I arrived, I felt I was a messenger delivering a bundle to the door, nothing more, delivering myself in a trauma of diminishment. I was a midget in my own mind and had managed to scramble safely through the flood of legs and arms threatening my destruction. I was safe, but I was not the same person as when I first started out. In my mind, I was diminished to myself, shrunken in my own eyes and worth little as a person or a factor in this teeming world. I could quickly die without causing the slightest hesitation in the steady flow of people on the walks.

It is inescapable to me that the human resides in the crowd motivated by ulterior drives; that the human resides in the man on the assembly line, in the mechanical murderer—in every kind of human experience, technological or otherwise. All derives from the imagination. If it is inconceivable to Sartre or Kierkegaard that an individual can be a human being as a fascist or in a crowd or as a murderer or rapist, then neither one has plumbed the really terrifying abyss that is humankind. To climb down those walls that are human, until the bottom is reached, where one has aged by then and is ready to be buried . . .

What should I do? Is there anything I should do, besides writing of my puzzlement? What must I do? What have I given myself to do as a must that I have conceived for myself, and if I have conceived of it for myself, on what basis? From what imperative source has this must arisen?

From myself, naturally. I conceived, from experience of the past, my life at home with my parents, my life in the street with friends. I have not thought it through as a system of values deriving from absolutes. My love for my parents was not absolute and neither was my love for my friends. Often I was bitter at them for failure to recognize my value, my thoughts, my reasoning, my crying need for recognition, and so I went out into the larger world without a definition for it or for myself. I acted as the main principle and that main principle, I began to see, was compounded of as many shadows as lights. I was neither an absolute believer in what I had lived through nor an absolute disbeliever. I wanted myself satisfied first, but how? I did not know what could satisfy me.

I am because I must be.

The memory of a dank, shadowy school gym on a hot summer day. I am standing at the entrance looking in, having walked from my house one-half mile away in search of friends or of something to do. The smell discouraged me, but worse was the fact that no one was present, and I walked back, first beginning to sense being alone and having nothing to do but feel my loneliness. What happened after that I can't recall, but it was enough. It cautioned me for the rest of that summer at least not to let myself get into such a situation again, and I can't recall whether or not I did avoid such a situation, but I know I was saddened by it and wondered whether this was to be my fate through life. I suddenly saw that empty, dank-smelling, shadowy gym as a metaphor of my existence, even of me as a person. I became identified in my mind with that image, and I carried it around with me silently and often subconsciously as the kind of person I was. It shadowed all my relationships from then on, and I became self-conscious about my self, my nature and strove, sometimes weakly, in despair with myself, sometimes happily when confidence was present for some reason, to overcome or transcend this conception of myself. I did not succeed very well, as I can recall, because my friendships appeared desultory to me—my fault, I would assume.

I did not give myself enough to these friendships. I was too withdrawn, dwelling upon that image of myself at the entrance

to the gym. Friends would look at me askance, as I imagined dur-
ing a silence between us, and depart with a short good-bye for
other and more interesting occupations than my lengthy silence.

Am I making all this up? I do remember chatting on about
baseball players, averages, team ratings, preferences among teams,
quarrels and rivalries between mutual friends, but it was all chatter
to me. I knew my real self was elsewhere and that my voice felt
strange to me in conversation about sports, and yet I did enjoy my
sports. I did not succeed at the games. I did want to win, and I
prided myself on being a very fast runner. De Fina was faster yet,
but I did not let it depress me. I knew I was faster than the other
boys, and that seemed compensation enough. But as for sitting
idly on a stoop with a friend and chatting of our opinions and
accomplishments in sports, that was okay as far as it could go but
how far was that? I'd feel the hollowness of it by comparison with
the solidity of that scary impression I had had of myself at the
gym. That was the key to my vision of myself and it extended to
all other areas besides sport and friendships. It went into my
thoughts of myself as a writer, as a son, as a lover. I became a man
looking dankly at life in shadow and wishing for sunshine all the
time, making poems about sunshine while living in shadow. I saw
Whitman as having done the same thing out of his perplexing life,
suddenly creating a poem of self-assurance and of confidence in
life and death, with him as a model, according to my view of him.
I wrote my poems, allowing myself bitter poems, only to be as-
sured in myself that they were part of a mosaic of work that would
include sweetness and gentleness and compassion for everyone.

This was not exactly what Whitman was about, but it served my
purpose then, to write so that I could embrace all of life rather
than dwell upon my inner sadness and shadow which, anyway, was
so easily refuted by the outward world of sunshine, trees, running
water, brilliant skies, laughing men and women arm in arm. I
believed in these outer things. They puzzled me in my sadness. I
enjoyed them and pursued them for myself also but never quite
succeeded in feeling them for myself personally, as I believed
others felt them for themselves. It was not much later in my life,

after marriage, that I began to suspect that others were experiencing my kind of sadness also, also experiencing a sense of deprivation about themselves and that the laughter and arm-in-arm walk with others held their sadness at bay. It was then that I began to grow more cheerful in myself, having learned or taught myself to believe that I had all this in common with others and that others were in my predicament too and that I was not so different, after all.

From dread of this loneliness as the mark of myself, I came to treasure it as my security and place of being, while the commonality I first hailed as a relief from my loneliness came to have an ambivalent meaning for me. While I needed it to feel myself not utterly alone and meaningless for that reason, it also held a threat to my being as I understand it now, that sense of apartness which always would be me. And so now I negotiate carefully between this self and the other to try to keep both in balance, without losing the value of either, if I can.

This desire or need for sleep that closed my eyes involuntarily as I read is to return to the peace of not knowing myself in sleep, not feeling myself and not feeling the world around me: all that we seek in social reform and political acts. I do it for myself without a party or a program or a social project funded by the state or private goodwilled liberal people who believe they have a debt of guilt to pay because they have apartments thirty stories up from dirt and killings and because they travel in closed cars to the country in summer where they can listen to the birds, instead of traffic and shootings. They have a debt to pay to those whose labor has spared them the life of the ordinary, and they act as if in the peace of sleep, as in a dream of goodwill, and they are happy with themselves, with much regret for the living. And when awake they confess that it is better to be dead for in their sense of debt is their appreciation of the death they have made for themselves.

The tree, does it perceive itself as we perceive ourselves? Because we usually think not. We look on the tree waving in the wind as something lifeless, given motion and form and leaves, and it is frightening because we would like to attribute to it those elements of life with which we associate life, such as growth and movement, and yet it does not appear to be so for the tree. There are forms of existence outside us that perform the acts of living and dying without being aware of themselves. They are of another order of existence that lives with us on the same planet, such as rocks too, and our first impulse is to rid the world of them, they are so frightening and remindful of death in life, exactly opposite our emphasis of life in death. Either rid the earth of them or perceive them as living things like ourselves. And we are not about to do it because they cannot communicate with us.

> *To me, the idea of line is virtually*
> *meaningless. One can break a line anywhere*
> *at all, and call a line of statistics "The line"*
> *itself. And so, I deal within these pages, much*
> *too many I'm sure, with the personal crisis*
> *and ruminations with which I am usually*
> *afflicted as a practicing, publishing poet.*
>
> —letter to the *Ohio Review*

1983–1984

In American life there is no transcendence. There is life and more life but no transcendence to yet another, different life. Anything else is a lie and pretension. What we have is the artist who can make something fine out of materials of his existence. That is the extent of our transcendence, long enough to last a day in the mind of the beholder, perhaps a bit longer in the mind of the artist, but even more: an encouragement to him to continue in this exercise at transcendence, once he is complimented, taken seriously.

To turn life into a means for art is about all we can and wish to do, but it is to make life known to us clearly, that which we are fated to live in and for the rest of our days.

Since writing in itself does not secure life, is not the elixir of immortality, I ask myself, why write, since it was for this purpose that I began to write? Why then write if it does not act for that purpose? And I have no answer beyond asking myself this question which, once asked, leaves me little more to say, if anything, and leaves me but to brood on the coming event and to see life as from the grave, its hopeless ending in darkness and forgetfulness of all that is beautiful in living, such as sex and art. "Why write?" persists as a question, as if an answer were somewhere hidden in the very question itself, that by asking it, it answers itself in the urgency with which the question is asked. In other words, the urgency to discover an answer for writing is the motive for writing which, of course, returns me to the original deceptive impulse to write, to attain through writing immortality. There is no giving up on the illusion that writing is the elixir of bodily immortality. If that is the case, then perhaps there is truth to it, at least for me, finding myself back where I started from in belief, in faith in my illusion, as if illusion by the very need to have it is truth itself. So says Stevens, and I believe it, the supreme fiction, which to me becomes more than fiction. It has become a fact of my reality, without which fact I have no reality.

Convince me that writing is not life itself, the body breathing, and I will confront a colorless world of leaves, faces, skies, a world entirely without color, everything a gray, and I begin to die, as though I had never been alive, something I do not believe as I die. Yes, I must believe, for as I believe new life stirs in me. I want to shout praise of living, joy of being, pleasure in self, glory of the earth. Writing takes on the act of all my praise, my pleasure and joy. Writing lives as I do, and it is not a lie or a deception to say writing contains the elixir that is life. Here in the writing it will last as long as men and women are here to read it, to become imbued with it, to rise like birds in flight from its lifted voice in praise.

Language as a person uses it signifies his or her educational background, home environment, social position, and political and philosophical beliefs. Therefore, language as I use it is that of the intellectual middle class, with no particular discipline of learning, simply a little of this and a little of that. It is language as used by average-educated businesspersons, reporters, teachers. I have a basic grasp of grammar that I and millions like myself try to adhere to.

This very writing is typical of my group. It is literate in the traditional sense and rooted in a bond of community with millions like myself who read the same newspaper and watch the same documentaries and dramas. It is not the language of specialization in any field. It is the language that tries to reach the broadest appeal. Therefore, it is neutral in tone, color, and rhetoric and nearly impersonal. It is this language that I use in my poetry, with the paradoxical effort to infuse this neutrality with its poetic surrogate in a search for what is at the bottom of my desire to base my poetry on such a plain speech. It is in one sense a conscious effort to appeal to the widest possible class of people, those like myself who do constitute a very wide representation of Americans. On the other hand, it is in an effort to ground my most private and complex thoughts in a rhetoric that can convey these thoughts and visions so that the reader may have the opportunity to identify with the poem. After all, I do believe there is more to us humans than our neutral language, that is, the language of society seeking a bridge among the vast majority. But its neutrality allows at the same time for color, tone, rhythm, and sound of the most personal and complex statement. In other words, it is open to change and manipulation through its own neutral cast. Individuation is another word for it.

If language could save me from death, I would already have been declared bodily immortal. I wrote with that thought in mind, thinking writing was an elixir of the secret of living forever, until I began to spy my hair graying. I had to acknowledge that if there is immortality, it is in writing itself as an art, not as an elixir of the body's survival.

Now I have to write so that what I write has the very breath of life itself, such as I can write into it to have it live beyond me, for me, by me, having by then died.

1985

The act of writing poetry is the act of being saved from illusions of friendships, love, and pity. It is the act of becoming without mercy for the self, which too is yet an illusion of becoming that is itself an illusion. The world never was anything but existent from the beginning, and flowers spring up out of the ground and die as quickly as becoming.

To write well inside oneself one needs strength, lots of it, and a need to use it in this art. Getting beneath the surface of self-satisfaction, pleasure in life, in friends, in food needs strength and determination, as if beneath the surface there is life, life at last, all else having been its prelude, its deception, its illusion; and what is beneath that surface? A whirling emptiness that is coming into being at one's own command, a being of emptiness into which everything fits and is poured so that it is all of life and yet a phantom of itself invested with emptiness. One pushes hard and as often delicately to make everything fit into this whirl of emptiness so that it looks as good inside this emptiness as it did on its outside, but there is this difference: that one has made of all these things an emptiness in each, as if they have come and gone, leaving only the forms they take in emptiness to attest to their having been. In its whirl of emptiness, one reads in such a poem that it is good, it is exciting, instructive. It releases the poet from his or her life. It makes the poet one with emptiness that now is everything, and he or she can celebrate the self in this emptiness too.

It works for that time of writing until the poet is through working and creating emptiness, when he or she must rise from the chair and begin to walk on solid wood floors and into solid sounds of cars and people, but emptiness is salvation. The poet has found the sense of his life and the life of everything else in emptiness. Things do not exist except as the poet makes them exist, but in this emptiness with which they are to be invested. They have become phantoms, controlled in the poet's self. The poet has the mastery. In the poem they are the poet's alone, but they can be read and resurrected by the reader too, for the reader too must need mastery, since like the poet, the reader is solid in hearing and appearance, which is the problem, as it is everyone's, and so the reader succeeds; the poet and the plain person, the person of pleasures and satisfactions and contentments, can find life in life, where the surface opens up to nothing, nothing at all.

1986

There is no meaning to the words we speak to one another, to the words we listen to on television. They serve only to indicate that we are in each other's presence, but as for what purpose, toward what end, for that we can find no clue in what we say to one another. It may mean that we need no purpose and no end in view. It may mean we exist for the sheer purpose of existing to one another. That would require another language, entirely new, perhaps impossible to write, since it would convey nothing other than its own physical presence, as unfortunately does the trivialized language we speak now. Perhaps we do not need a language between us if it is enough that we see, hear, and live with one another. At least, we would not be pretending that we are communicating ideas, sympathies, and so on, that are not there in what we say to one another.

We would not be pretending, and that, at least, is good, so that language, new language, could be a babble to affirm to us that it makes no difference what we say. It never says what we think we want to say. Am I going too far? To write coherently and to communicate means we are conditioned by the way of feeling, seeing, hearing, thinking, and acting, to be heard and read as coherent and communicating, but the fact of the matter is that no two persons can agree on what is being said, heard, read, or done, despite that "coherence and clarity." In fact, it is just this coherence and clarity that lends itself to this multiplicity of interpretation by the very fact of its neutral speech.

In other words, I am discouraged at the style I have formed for myself of clarity and coherence. I cannot make myself understood as I had intended to be understood, and yet I can say for a fact that as I look back upon my poems they convey what I myself attempted to say, or must I admit that I am discovering new meanings in them from what I had originally believed they were intended to mean?

So where am I in all this as a poet? Do I move over to the "Language poets" who know this problem intimately? Do I begin to write outside the conventions of clarity and coherence so that at least in incoherence deliberately done I am making a statement that communication as we think we can communicate does not exist? Where does that leave me? It leaves me wanting to write in the spirit of the "Language poets," as I may well try:

> There is rain in the street.
> Yesterday I shopped for two hours.
> I am going for a walk.
> I saw you in the mirror
> standing behind me.
>
> Also, it was dark.
> Also, what do you do for a living?
> Also, is there a time
> when you are free?
> Also, I like ice cream,
> but not that much.

Is this the only way we can attack the conventions of feeling, and so on, that we have agreed upon socially, politically, and culturally? What do we have in mind with which to replace these conventions? I don't think opacity is the answer. Yet we do not have a whole new set of conventions with which to oppose the present conventions. The new must come organically out of the negation we bring to the old, must emerge out of its own negation of the past by recognizing a vacuum as the old conventions begin to disintegrate under attack. To fill a vacuum will be the start of the new conventions, and conventions they will be eventually, as they fill all the vacancies left by the collapse of the old, because life must be continued, since it was life renewed, refreshed, that was the motive for the rebellion against outmoded, outworn, jaded conventions. We will have begun a new era of thought, feeling, acts, and beliefs, only to discover that we are also fostering a rebellion once again, an inevitable occurrence in the light and inspiration of the victory over the old. Nevertheless, it must happen, and it will happen that the present will give way to the yet more immediate present and forever, as long as we inhabit this world alive.

₰ 25. Life, Now and Forever ₰

I can't imagine what there is to say about a holocaust that will leave no one and nothing alive. To write about that is as if to actually contemplate and look forward to its happening. At least that is how I feel about it. I prefer not to think of the event at all, since I refuse to believe it will happen. I still believe in the sanity of the human race in the face of such ultimate disaster. I still believe that survival is the key to our thinking, man, woman, and child, red, white, black, yellow, or what have you. Survival is what will be uppermost in our minds in a crisis, if it ever comes to that, and we will survive by finding a path between us on which each of us can travel to and from one another, if not as sworn friends at least as sworn survivors. Whether friendship will emerge from that among the political and racial differences I would not predict, but at least we will understand that we cannot survive alone at the cost of the death of others, that that period in history is gone with the election of nuclear war as the weapon.

We will have to live with one another, tolerating each other's prejudices, gripes, biases, eccentricities, and anything else that puts off one people from another, one race from another, one religion from another. But think of the kind of world in which we stare into each other's faces, faces of those that we would rather have massacred the day before the nuclear weapon was created. What an awkward situation it will be for us all: the communists who can't stand the belly of the capitalists swollen there before them with good solid beef and potatoes, and the capitalists who will have to look steadily and passively at the communists who once planned to do away with them. Neither will have even a sidearm in possession, but they will stare at each other and, who knows, perhaps

begin grouchily talking to one another, each conceding that there
has to be something human about the other, who can speak to the
point, grimace, laugh (harshly), tell a crude joke on the other,
spit on the floor in contempt, but then look up at the opponent and
smile helplessly because this is as far as either can go in deriding
the other, negating the other physically or mentally; and I dream
they will laugh at and with each other for finding themselves in
this ridiculous cul de sac. Will they begin to chat a bit about living
conditions, the weather, their respective leaders? Tell each other
jokes in confidence about politics, jokes that each had withheld in
private in the past but that now are harmless enough in the face of
the nuclear threat?

And since they will have already conceded that the nuclear
bomb cannot be used, won't they begin to think seriously of de-
activating them all and starting all over again by making just ordi-
nary rifles and cannon? Or, miracle of miracles, will it occur to
both of them at the same time that they don't need weapons at all
from now on, since they have begun to trade jokes with each other,
on politics especially?

It's difficult to go beyond this vision, in the face of the crisis of
the present, but it is the vision I'd like to hold on to as the one that
gives me the most confidence that we will prevail in spite of and
perhaps because of our foolishness. We will begin to sense the
stupidity of dying wholesale off the face of the earth when the
earth has so much to offer us in the way of benefits for living, and
I think I'm not alone in holding on to the vision I have because
so many of us are silent in the face of this crisis, communing with
the vision of the ultimate sanity of survival, even as it makes us
pull back from our self-righteousness and self-approval to see our-
selves as fools to have threatened our very own existence in threat-
ening that of our opponent.

I'm at that age when the thought of death is uppermost in mind.
I think about the life that those I leave behind will be living, sur-
rounded by arsenals of neutron bombs, and I wonder what worth

there will be for them in living under the constant threat of anni-
hilation. I also think of the men and women in power today, many
of whom are of my age and with children whom they will leave
behind, as I will. Isn't it possible, I ask myself, that they could be
thinking my thoughts also, asking themselves the same question in
sight of the arsenals they have built up everywhere on the earth?
Do they not, like me, realize the horror of leaving behind all of
this mass threat to life itself for their children to live with? Is there
no sense of guilt, remorse, nausea that their lives have been spent
in creating the condition for the most awful imaginable catas-
trophe, the total destruction of the earth and its people? Surely
they are seeking a way out of the maze of terror. I simply cannot
conceive of these men not thinking and trying to rid the world of
this threat. Surely they are all men with normal desires for the
perpetuation of their kind in their family, relatives, pets, homes,
cities, gardens, lakes. Can we not then hope for their cautious and
prayerful approach to the problem, as we raise our voices with
theirs so that it becomes a universal supplication—to whom but to
ourselves so that we will turn upon ourselves to realize we are our
own guarantee of safety and perpetuity? In this I see a world gov-
ernment finally emerging out of the necessity of keeping ourselves
alive and our hopes for our children realized in their freedom from
fear. I believe this is the only thing that can rescue us from total
destruction by our own hands.

As for the major political, social, economic issues of today, when
the leading nations begin to realize that all these problems are
inextricably bound up with the safety of the world from nuclear
disaster, we will begin to see a measured, sane, and reasoned ap-
proach to the solution of each of these issues. Until then, we can-
not hope for solutions at all.

As for reflection upon these issues in the art I practice, these
issues inevitably are reflected in the mood I bring to personal prob-
lems and in personal problems that I see are inextricably bound
up with social, political, and economic problems nationally and
internationally. We have become one world, but so many still

cannot concede that the inevitable has happened. Still, there is no clear-cut need to write of these issues in their literal sense, since as poets we write out of the world that we create with language and that world of language is never a simple world of "issues." It is rather a world as absolute in itself for each writer as the language creates, with its own referential keys, guides, and directions that have arisen in the person from conditioning, training, and innate capacity for language; so that, as each of us emerges as writer from his or her environment, he or she has the stamp of a unique person. It can happen that a writer will be able to write authentically of issues in the style that is the mark of this writer's world. Bertolt Brecht was such a writer, but it doesn't follow that each of us must model ourselves upon his style, and yet each of us knows full well how deeply affected we are by the whole range of problems that afflict the earth, and so each of us works within the capacities given us to express, communicate the very source of our private concerns. Thus, the relation between the social/political/economic issues and one's art is never a one-to-one relationship, and yet every poet's art has within it these elements that can be traced to social/political/economic conditioning and practice and are expressive of those issues in terms of his or her personal art. There is no other way for an artist whose one function, ultimately, is to create his or her own world of perception, understanding, and spirituality. It is never a life and art totally divorced from the lives of others. It is a contribution to the life of the whole earth in its confounding variety, and so adds to the one voice of the cry, Life, now and forever.

26. The Right to Renew

Two men are standing on the roof opposite my window and looking down into the courtyard. They have a view of my window and may be looking down at me at my typewriter. My first impulse is to get up and pull down the shades. I am embarrassed that they find me at my most secluded and trying time and can look down with the equanimity of strangers. What could they know of the struggle one goes through to write, to get out of one's system the tension, the hostility, and aggression that motivate one's writings? I could be a madman to them or a fantastic fool who truly thinks himself his own best physician, one who finds himself his own best friend—the mark of adolescence, immaturity, me at forty, or *sixty*. They would see me, in their minds, at play, wasting my good time and energy in superfluous, unproductive work. True, all persons retain aggressions and hostilities in themselves, and all persons, or at least most brought up in the ways of civilization, find other and more productive and useful ways to release themselves. They hold jobs, they raise families, keep gardens, drive cars, join societies, entertain guests; do a hundred and one things that will sublimate or compensate or relieve their tensions in harmless ways, so long as they are approved by others. But who approves of a writer who sits down and seeks to be his own cure through writing? It is a form of self-pity at best, they suspect. It is a mark of a retarded personality, so the doctors say. Others stay by themselves for pleasure. Alone, they either must have a book, a telephone, or a television set handy, and not especially in that order—an object outside themselves into which they may enter or with which they may amuse themselves or free themselves of the tensions that accumulate when one is alone. Drink, too, is a form of release, and all these are approved methods. But if one attempts to draw from oneself the necessary relief—that is held suspect of abnormality and an aberration. The hobbyist is approved of; one who builds boats, airplanes, pantry shelves, or who grows gardens or collects stamps is respected as a member of society. But to the writer, writing is no hobby. The hobbyist deprived of his or her stamp collection eventually will turn to what else is close at hand, bottle tops or corkscrews. The writer without the opportunity to write feels deprived of air.

It is this seriousness with which the writer approaches writing that makes him or her suspect to the good citizen, who cannot understand or may even refuse to understand. To be serious as a writer means to withdraw from what is equally serious to the good citizen, the ways of existence among one's own kind: the habits, the routines, the ceremonies, and the practices of the majority of the population. The serious writer withdraws from these events and happenings to spend unseemly long hours at his or her own practices. This constitutes a challenge to the good citizen, who is right in suspecting its motivation in the writer.

The writer approaches his typewriter when in that desperate mood as a rebel, as a man challenging every concept ever held. All to him is as nothing now. He is driven by a mood that can find little satisfaction in the ordinary rituals of life, such as going to the movies or entertaining or driving a car or taking pleasure in business or even marriage. He can find no release for his pent-up feelings in any of the modes by which others satisfy themselves. He must, it seems, begin from the beginning all over again. It may lead to the construction of an entirely new set of ideas about one's life so that it becomes upsetting to all those who come in contact with it. To the writer who has had the pleasure and relief of forming himself anew from the chaotic mood in which he found himself at the start, his new thoughts may proclaim a fresh and livelier existence, not only for himself but for all his contemporaries. Heedless of the shock his thoughts may bring, he goes about publishing them in the faith that he is doing his part as an aspiring citizen.

Why is the writer afflicted with this need constantly to renew his vision and judgment of things as they are? He holds within, perhaps even against his own better judgment, this recurrent torment that for the lack of any other name he describes as the creative urge. It is creative only in the process of destroying. From where and why does he, along with other artistic persons, derive this terrible drive? He may look from heaven to earth for the explanation only to find it in what he beholds. We do not remain satisfied with ourselves when confronted with the phenomenon of the earth and sky. We are driven to frustration by their immensity and stillness, by their apparent indestructibility and immortality. One grows acutely aware of one's own limitations as a human being, a walking, eating, drinking, sleeping, loving creature who deprived of any one of these practices for long must give up his life, too. He is the embodiment of weakness and tentativeness, while the earth and sky abide forever in their forms. How then can he go about for long satisfied with this or that routine in his life, as if it could secure all that one is or make one as durable as the mountain? These are palpable impossibilities that escape no one, hardly less the most hidebound ritualist among us. The writer is more keenly aware than anyone else because, having affirmed the truth of the situation, as has the rest of the world in its way, he is unable to evade it, as so many others do, consciously or unconsciously. To the writer remains the peculiar trait of being caught in his own vision, spellbound by the truth. The writer is the vulnerable one who, unlike others, has not found it possible to overcome the blow that was first struck in youth. Others have found it possible, either by strength or evasive tactics, to exert themselves in another direction that will take them away for a period of their lives from that first staggering insight. The writer remains fixed to the spot in which he has been found. It is a kind of flaw of which the world is well aware in itself, for if the writer, as though in convulsion, seeks from time to time to renew himself and his thought in order to feel refreshed and at one again with the world, it is merely the manifestation of the world itself in its cycle of life and death and rebirth. Nature remains constant apart from us. We must die and we begin to die with the deepening of every system of thought and life into a habit or ritual. In truth, the writer is no rebel but acts to proclaim his right to renew himself while there is life. He will not say he does it for everyone. The task of renewal belongs to those who seek to read his work or do so by accident. But what he does for himself he does not overlook as an aid to others, and if you will ignore him or laugh at him or seek to suppress him he will know that you will have recourse to him in time, with an even greater need.

Those two men upon the roof have vanished, but in their absence have given me good cheer, and so I thank all those who stand upon rooftops looking down upon us, the writers.

Epilogue
As Long as Life Matters

I believe, as do most of us, with certain exceptions, which I'll get to later, that poetry is personal in origin. Why not, then, trace the roots of my poetry so as to bestow an authenticity on this search for the absolute and, because most of us do agree that poetry is personal in origin, my tale and conclusion to it should, if not in detail, at least by implication, apply to the experience of nearly all of us. In brief, we do make up some sort of family among us, but what kind of family is the subject of this talk and my autobiographical account.

I will begin with the story of an experience I had in my midfifties, an experience that now finds itself confronted by a deeply troubled and divided present in poetry. There I sat in my car, waiting for a red traffic light to turn green. As I recall it now, I was mulling over a statement I had read several days earlier maintaining that no scientific experiment can be purely objective, the factor of the observing scientist having to be included as a variable. As this statement hovered in my mind, I made an elated leap to connect it with the writing of poetry. The individual, as I already knew to my sorrow, is the significant factor in poetry too, but suddenly at the wheel of my car I felt myself completely free to write as I pleased, as if I had not been doing so from the start, and now I was released from a long-standing guilt about it.

Why this guilt, and where did it come from? There is the popular explanation for it: We poets do not contribute to the wealth, health, comfort, and longevity of the people and, often, not to our own either, and thus the personal dilemma, at least for most of us.

This experience in my mid-fifties, however, did have its roots in the early days of my upbringing, which I will get to now to make this particular moment understandable. It began in the family. I was raised with two younger sisters, all of us, parents and children, bound in love and respect for each other. However, as I reconstruct it now, it was all predicated on the understanding that we gave respect and love to the family itself, meaning that one could not act outside the family without expecting to be looked on with some apprehension. Our every act had to be in the interest and welfare of us all. These family ties with one another were indeed strong, to be violated only at the deepest traumatic cost to ourselves, as I was to know in a short time.

I was my father's favorite, aglow in his loving approval of me. On my thirteenth birthday, that time in the Jewish religion of confirmation of one's arrival at adult responsibilities and duties, I asked for and received his approving permission to write my own acceptance speech. This sign of trust from my father clinched my unspoken wish to become a writer, yet almost immediately after, with the onset of the Great Depression, as I have said, we became bitterly alienated from each other when he demanded that I enter his business to work a twelve-hour shift, replacing another worker in order to buy food for the family. I was acutely aware of the problems he confronted, but I was also experiencing, in my own outrage, a sense of his betrayal of me. On one level I knew my anger to be unreasonable, but on another I felt justified, not alone because of his past approval and support, but also because I believed he was betraying himself, which meant he was betraying me too. I found I had become deeply identified with him.

I was not without guilt at my determined stand against joining him in his business; I was angry too because of my feeling of guilt; it threatened to undermine and destroy my resolve not to submit to an exhausting, destructive twelve-hour shift. Bound in with this resolve was my effort to rescue and affirm that part of my father I yet believed in and loved, that part that was myself in him. I soon found I was isolated within the family, its support withdrawn from me. Bitter as was my loss, even more anguishing was to witness the one person I had looked to for his authority on behalf of my ambition, that person hostile to that very life he had encouraged in me. Defiantly, I became my own authority and support.

And so to write began to mean to me to go against that one mainstay that had nurtured me in my ambition, my ambition having helped to undermine that mainstay, my guilt and anguish compounded and now as much directed toward myself as toward my father. I little before this time I had begun to read Whitman. It was as if I found in him a correspondence to all I believed was the life I was then living within my family, or so I thought. In reaction to my break with my father and in a kind of excited depression, I made Whitman my surrogate father, his poems becoming my supportive family, yet with a sense of guilt still strong within me.

Witness again the sudden exhilaration at my release from guilt in my mid-fifties, which I recounted earlier, its affirming the individual freely for me. And yet there was to be a paradox, one I am about to relate that developed in later years and which impels this discussion toward its conclusion. However, to tell of this event will also help set the record straight about my final relationship with my father, in itself the crux of this paradox. Years after my angry departure from home, he had begun to prosper and even to take pride in me as a poet, but sadly, there was no way I could restore in myself his once overriding authority. Love me he did, but his advice, guidance, and moral support did not exist for me any longer. He was an ordinary man, and I no longer counted myself as any different either, considering the ordinary circumstances we now both faced of marriage, work, love, and fatherhood. I could see that both of us were subject to the same dilemmas of existence, which were without real solutions beyond what we could salvage through our own efforts and will. Ironically, it was an existence inner directed and, therefore, shaky, subject to the unpredictable and the unaccountable that assailed us from without as well as from within. I had to look beyond my father—and myself—for the truth.

In my belated acknowledgment that writing poetry was in es-

sence to act as an autonomous person, free in oneself, with the
freedom to celebrate, I published that 1971 essay "The Necessity
of the Personal," in which I praised the virtues and strengths of the
poet, as an individual, of encompassing significance for poetry, and
for life itself. Here, I believed, I had found the absolute of which
I had been in search ever since the break with my father and that
now I saw to be an extension or development of the Whitman
theme that I had for so long depended on, albeit ambivalently.
Now its authority for me was grounded in the universality of the
condition of the autonomous being. Wherever I turned I saw poets
writing out of their own lives with a conviction and authority of
their own that was both admirable and persuasive of the truth that
I had only recently learned to embrace. And now I was among
these poets, once more in a family, but this time of my own choos-
ing and bent.

I wrote steadily and with confidence, free in myself at last to do
so. What was it that awoke me, not very much later, to a reality
other than this confident one, which began a shift in my mood
away from this supportive companionship that I had found in the
writing of poetry? Why this change? What was its character? And
why a troubling, renewed sense of guilt and anger on yet a new
plane, one difficult to absorb and to transcend, since it resided in
the very nature of my relationship to poetry and to my fellow
poets? I ask myself these questions to find an explanation and, if
possible, a remedy. I ask myself: If all of us, as I had believed,
were united in the common goal of realizing ourselves through
poetry, what causes a division among us? Who, if anyone, is re-
sponsible? Could it be that as individuals we must distinguish our-
selves from each other by acts of hostility, indifference, and dis-
dain?

I can understand this painful new development as in part a re-
action to the excesses by some poets in their concentration on per-
sonal issues—so much that is trivial, inconsequential, or without
form, taste, or reason for being other than to show itself as the
poetry of the self. William Carlos Williams was caustic in his re-

marks about such sloppy work. So much poor writing may have signaled to certain American critics a breakdown in American poetry and as a result may have triggered the sharp reaction to which we are witness today. I am not about to name these critics or raise issues, since my point is to let these names and issues be reflected in the divisions among us, so that I may concentrate on the effect rather than on the causes, which we know. My reason for that decision will be clear enough as I progress in what I have to say. I am here to speak of myself as perhaps representative of those who feel threatened in their beliefs and practices and betrayed, as it seems, by exactly those critics I have just alluded to who claim their authority from Whitman. Of course, we would much prefer to accept a learned, sensitive authority and be at one with it in the endeavor to adapt Whitman to our contemporary needs, but what can we say when we find ourselves confronted by hostility, as if, in our need to claim Whitman too, we were trespassing on private property?

This is not an emotional issue alone; I am also speaking of those paradoxes and ironies to which I earlier referred. I honor those same critics for their belated appreciation of Whitman, he whom I and many others have been reading and writing to and about for nearly fifty years while he was yet being ignored, often ridiculed, by those very institutions and their academicians who now have raised him to an eminence among us. But is there still not the possibility that we will find Whitman in the basement once again in some not too distant future? It's as if he has been made a means with which to exclude from recognition those same poets, such as Robert Bly, George Oppen, James Wright, Gary Snyder, and Robert Creeley, to name only a few who derive from Whitman.* Is this not already a disguised form of hostility toward Whitman?

So now, for those like myself, our guilt attendant on our rejec-

---

* All five have since received at least a portion of recognition with their induction into the National Institute of Arts and Letters or "lesser" forms of esteem.

tion of those critical voices that we would have preferred to call our own, we carry on, once more having to realize we are our own authority and support; that there are no fathers among us; that we must make do with ourselves.

Unquestionably, we need comments, observations, and critiques but certainly not so as to divide the poets from each other with self-important judgments, as though separating sheep from goats. We do not need shepherds of that breed, especially not those who claim to elevate criticism to an aesthetic position and mode equal to, if not superior to, poetry itself. What more do we need to demonstrate the disarray among poets today than such a claim that sets poets against critics and poets against poets, as the critics preside in judgment among us as in lordly domain. Where is Whitman in this?

I am in agreement that there must be change, at the same time that I am reminded that it carries within itself its own cause, so that, as it absorbs the past, it must also struggle against it to exist as change. Thus it cannot deny or reject the past, without losing its own character. We do not as yet kill off our parents and grandparents, except perhaps by forgetting they exist, only to remind ourselves of them as we ourselves begin to age.

The Poetics of Indeterminacy, by Marjorie Perloff, reminds me that it was a reaction to certainties, assurances, and blandishments that triggered the revolution among early twentieth-century poets, such as Eliot and Pound, who brought with them the then explosive power of their doubts, ambiguities, and rejections. And when I read about Deconstructionism, it reminds me of the Marxist campaign of the early thirties and mid-forties that sought to bludgeon the so-called bourgeois poets into conforming with Marxist theory and practice by denouncing those poets as submissive to the demands and needs of capitalism and imperialism. In other words, the Marxists sought to strip these poets of their own uniquely personal commitments and contributions. In turn, the poets, once stripped of their individuality, were to become instruments for accomplishing the revolution. Now we have the theory, to put it as simply as possible, that no writer exists uniquely in himself or herself but again is the voice tuned to the voice of his or her culture, and this is given to us in the dress of intellectual probity, scholarship, and deeply keen self- and societal analysis. Do we need a repetition of the earlier orthodoxy in its latest academic dress?

We should welcome indeterminacy as a restatement of Pound's dictum, "Make It New." In making it new, we find our language perforce indeterminate, especially as to how and what to say that can set itself in contrast to the tried and worn. A tone of resistance to the old and tried becomes the clue to the new, as the new works to emerge in full strength and meaning. This is what I want to save, this effort at renewal. This is what is under attack, the voice that does not conform to literary criteria given from on high.

In brief, I am making a plea for a certain tolerance for what is emerging, but with a plea for respect too for what has made possible that which is emerging. There are no longer absolute criteria for judgment, not even in oneself. That is one of the surprising and troubling conclusions I have come to, and so in a way I agree with Deconstructionism, for the individual is in doubt today, exactly as there are no set judgments as to what is and what is not true. That pertains to the nature of poetry too. It is simply as protean as is life itself, but one survives and writes with all that is a spur to writing, as if in defiance, as if to distinguish onself from the chaos. That is where absolute judgment may be made—the poet discovering for himself or herself a form or order that is yet free to change into still another shape and sound. And so I welcome in myself those poets and critics who are at work seeking to express the emerging new, its indeterminacy in relation to the old and the tensions arising from the introduction of the indeterminate, a situation that we have seen and experienced in recent past literary eras and that continues in character with our times. We must not forget that without each other we lack significance in ourselves. We need one another if only to become distinguished in ourselves from each other in our right and reason. This is an absolute I cling to, and it gives me much pleasure. It is family once again.

Yet I wish to add as an afterthought some remarks that round out and complete an initially private experience on the subject of the absolute. It begins as follows:

It's never possible for me, for one, to give any fixed account of what I'm trying to do as a poet; it varies so with the circumstances in which I find myself. At one moment I may be thinking of writing the definitive account of the spirit since Christ; at another time I will want to incorporate in my poems every theory Freud developed; at still another time I am involved in my daily routine life, with time for love or pleasure or domestic tranquility, and yet I can't totally forswear these plunges into the absolute, which I am susceptible to.

The absolute is my deepest preoccupation, which naturally I, like everyone else, must fail at and in my path through life must trust that this preoccupation will bring me to some revelation that will stay with me until eternity beyond the grave. I am serious. I want, as poet, to speak the whole truth and nothing but the truth, so help whoever or whatever is there to whom or to which I may swear my faith. Let it or who listen or not, I will make my allegiance clear and unequivocal. I want an absolute revelation but also want my daily existence, so how do I mediate between them? Is mediation possible? This conflict too lies beneath the surface of my wish for the absolute and, as I can guess, undermines, dilutes, circumscribes, and disintegrates it, the sad, sad part of this ambivalent existence.

I am ready for death. Is that the final absolute revelation? So be it. I know of no other certain event that could bring its own truth with it, and if this is what I am looking for, then a welcome to it. I write of death often, and it may be that I have not been aware that the revelation has been with me for all this while, ever since I can remember, as far back as my childhood when I stood leaning against the gate of a cemetery and looked out into the sky and spoke to it, as if it were listening, as if it were the being to whom I should address myself in wonder. I was answered from within by the emergence of a poem.

Since then, death has been a stimulus to my work. Is that not a revelation, seeing myself in the perspective of death, which speaks to me clearly of my life? I turn to my life and write about it with the exactness that love demands. Love, of course, because it is love that the imminence of death stirs in me for life, and when I am finally quit of life I will, again I hope, have written only with love of the ugly, the critical, the angry and sarcastic, equally with the tender to persons and to life itself. Death is this two-faced Gorgon, for death is my theme, but life is my subject, and I smile on everyone.

And so here I have just given a firm account of what I am doing as a poet, I who am so full of contradictions, but the pleasure is mine in having discovered an absolute that, I know, I will forget or pass through in time and other circumstances than this in which I am now writing. Yet I should tell myself over and over that there are no absolutes, if I keep finding absolutes in every alley and crossroads of my life. I should say that each absolute is for its time, and let it go at that. I should be content with that, and yet, though I have told myself this repeatedly, I cannot rest with that thought. I keep searching, restless, afraid that I am missing something so obvious, that is staring me in the face, something that could give me my sense of immortality. For it's immortality I want when I seek after the absolute, to discover and grasp it between my hands, to win it over into my body, to make my body an absolute too, immortal.

Am I afraid to face and acknowledge that which is being told me throughout my changeful life and thought—that there are no absolutes and that alone is the final one on which to rest my search? How celebrate, enjoy, and live in the pleasure of that discovery? By acknowledging my own limits, but somehow through this changefulness in me to be identified with that which is forever. I must bow my head and live as long as life matters.

Index

❧ Acknowledgments ❧

Many of the chapters in this book appeared previously in somewhat different form: "The Formative Years" in *Contemporary Authors Autobiography Series,* III (Gale Publishers, 1986); "Living with Change" in *Literature and the Urban Experience* (Rutgers University, 1981); "Surrealist Interlude" and "Robert Bly" in *Poetry East* (1982 and 1981); "Your Child as Writer" in *Poets & Writers Magazine* (1987); "My Life with Whitman" in *West Hills Review* (1979); "Finding William Carlos Williams" in *Unmuzzled Ox* (1981); "William Carlos Williams and Wallace Stevens: Two of a Kind" in *American Poetry Journal* (1986); "Charles Reznikoff" in *Partisan Review* (1977) and *Charles Reznikoff: Man and Poet* (Milton Hindus, ed., National Poetry Foundation Inc., 1984); "Charles Olson" in *Street Magazine;* "Louis Zukofsky" in *Paideuma* (1978); "Stanley Kunitz" in *Antaeus* (1980); "Paul Zweig" in Poetry Society of America *Newsletter* (1984); "Simon Perchik" in *Who Can Touch These Knots* by Simon Perchik (Scarecrow Press, 1985); "Not One Voice but Many" in *American Poetry* (1987); "A Poet Is Not Autonomous" in *South Dakota Review* (1967); "The Self and the Other" in *Ironwood* (1983); "All Else Is Prelude" in *The Ohio Review* (1987); "Life, Now and Forever" in *TriQuarterly* (1981); "Epilogue: As Long as Life Matters" as "In Search of an Absolute" in *What Is a Poet?* (Hank Lazer, ed., University of Alabama, 1987), copyright © 1987 by the University of Alabama, reprinted with permission.

About the Author

David Ignatow has won a number of awards for his poetry—the Bollingen Prize in 1977, and, earlier, two Guggenheim fellowships, the Wallace Stevens fellowship from Yale University, the Rockefeller Foundation fellowship, the Shelley Memorial Award, and the National Institute of Arts and Letters award. He was poet in residence at Walt Whitman's birthplace in 1987. He is president emeritus of the Poetry Society of America.

Since 1964 Ignatow has taught at the New School for Social Research, the University of Kentucky, the University of Kansas, Vassar College, York College of the City University of New York, and New York University. He is now adjunct lecturer at Columbia University. He was an editor of *The American Poetry Review*, 1972–1976; *Chelsea Magazine*, 1967–1972; *The Nation*, 1962–1963; *The Beloit Poetry Journal*, 1949–1959; and *Analytic*, 1936–1938. He is the author of thirteen books of poetry and two other prose books. He lives in East Hampton, Long Island.

About the Book

The One in the Many is composed in Linotype Garamond No. 3. Garamond was introduced in America by American Type Foundry in 1919, when their cutting, based on the *caractères de l'Université* of the Imprimerie Nationale, appeared. Many other versions were made for Linotype, Monotype, Intertype, Ludlow, and the Stempel foundry. The face has since been adapted for phototypesetting, CRT typesetting, and laser typesetting.

The book was composed by Yankee Typesetters of Concord, New Hampshire, and designed by Kachergis Book Design of Pittsboro, North Carolina.

Wesleyan University Press, 1988